WILLIAM BERRY HARTSFIELD

WILLIAM BERRY HARTSFIELD
Mayor of Atlanta

HAROLD H. MARTIN

Athens
THE UNIVERSITY OF GEORGIA
PRESS

Copyright © 1978 by the University of Georgia Press
Athens 30602

Set in 11 on 14 point Caledonia type
Printed in the United States of America

Library of Congress Cataloging in Publication Data
Martin, Harold H.
    William Berry Hartsfield, Mayor of Atlanta.
    Includes bibliographical references and index.
    1. Hartsfield, William Berry. 2. Atlanta—
Mayors—Biography. 3. Atlanta—Politics and
government. I. Title.
F294.A853H375 975.8′231′040924 [B] 78-1550
            ISBN 0-8203-0445-X

Grateful acknowledgment is given to the Atlanta
Historical Society and to Special Collections,
Robert W. Woodruff Library, Emory University,
for permission to reproduce the photographs used
in this book.

He's got a hot temper, a stinging tongue, a strong will, a quick wit, a kind heart, a sense of history, a sense of destiny, a sense of humor, a capacity for growth, and a built-in finely tuned political radar set that seldom has failed him in his public life.

Atlanta Journal
June 7, 1961

CONTENTS

ILLUSTRATIONS

ACKNOWLEDGMENTS

For help and encouragement in preparing this biography of William B. Hartsfield, I am deeply indebted to many who knew him not only as mayor but as a volatile, vital, and complex man. I am grateful to William L. Pressly and Franklin Garrett of the Atlanta Historical Society, for conceiving and sponsoring such a book, and for making working space and all the Hartsfield materials in the society's archives available to me—including, of course, that infallible source, Mr. Garrett's own book *Atlanta and Environs.* I owe an equal debt of gratitude to David Estes and Linda Matthews of the Special Collections in the Robert W. Woodruff Library at Emory University, where an even more voluminous compilation of Hartsfield memorabilia may be found, placed there by his widow. The extremely able staff of the Atlanta Public Library, which Hartsfield considered his alma mater, was also helpful.

Especially am I grateful to those who knew and loved Bill Hartsfield as a human being as well as a politician—to Mildred Hartsfield Cheshire, his daughter, whose insights were invaluable to me, and to Robert Woodruff, his oldest friend and strongest supporter. And particularly am I grateful to Tollie Bedenbaugh Hartsfield, who married him as he came to the end of his career as mayor, for her memories of those years which she made warm and bright for him with love and understanding.

For many insights into his stormy temperament and his sturdy character, I am indebted to journalists who knew him in his active years and who shared their judgments with me. They were many and frank-spoken. Gene Patterson, Bill Emerson, Joe Cumming, Jake Carlton, John Crown, Pat Watters, Raleigh Bryans—all were helpful. Nor would I conclude this list of those to whom I am indebted without mentioning my gratitude to Malcolm MacDonald of the University of Georgia Press, for sound counsel and advice, and to Karen Orchard, for skillful editing which gave pace and movement to my sometimes turgid prose.

Harold Martin

INTRODUCTION

"ALL CITIES are the loneliness of man," the poet said.[1] And so they are. But cities, too, represent the dreams and hopes of men, the goals of men, the lust for proud achievement in all fields—in business, in education, in industry, and in the arts.

Cities are first the product of their geography. They are what they are because of where they are and what is there—their riches in minerals, timber, soil, and water. Atlanta first became a great city because of its location at a natural crossing point for a national network of railroads. It became an even greater city because its leaders were determined that in the age of flight Atlanta, not Birmingham, should be the great southeastern regional terminal and crossing point for a national and international network of airlines.

Cities, therefore, can reach their full potential only when to their natural advantages is added the genius of talented and farsighted men, firmly resolved to make fullest use of those resources. And in that respect, Atlanta has been fortunate. Through the changing years since its incorporation in 1847, Atlanta has had its periods of weak and corrupt leadership. But on the whole the men who have guided it from the mayor's seat in City Hall have been men of honor and vision, spurred by a deep conviction of their city's proud destiny. Norcross, Calhoun, Williams, English, Hillyer, Hemphill, Mims, Howell,

Maddox, Candler, Key, Allen—they survive in the memory, and in the names of buildings, streets, and schools.

Among them, though, one man stands out above all others. The late William Berry Hartsfield first became mayor of Atlanta in 1937, and from then until he retired in 1961, except for a brief wartime period, he was its chief executive. And in all that quarter century there was hardly a moment, day or night, when his thoughts were not upon the problems and the promise of his city. He kept it clean, he kept it honest, he kept it growing bigger, busier, and more beautiful year by year. It was a part of him, and he of it, man and municipality being of one mind and spirit.

When he retired as mayor in 1961, the scruffy depression-haunted city he had taken over in 1937 had doubled in population to nearly half a million and had tripled in land area. It had become the third most populous capital city in the nation and the cultural, commercial, and financial center of a five-county metropolitan area of more than a million people. To the retiring mayor this was no surprise. "Atlanta," he told an interviewer, "is a city of destiny whose growth has hardly begun."[2]

The decade of the sixties proved him right. When he died in 1971 after ten vigorous and active years in retirement, the city he had loved and fought for was the center of a metropolis of 1,390,000 people and covered more than 1,700 square miles. At its heart was downtown Atlanta, whose spectacular new buildings made a memorable sight from the great expressways approaching the city's center.

He always argued that no civic project should be named for a living man. As a result, when he died, a week before his eighty-first birthday, only two things had been named in his honor—"Willie B.," a baby ape at the Grant Park Zoo, and the city incinerator. The naming of the airport "Hartsfield International" was to come later, when he could no longer object. But his town had not forgotten him in his private years. In the funeral cortege that passed from Spring Hill to West View Cemetery, with a pause in tribute at City Hall, rode all the leaders of the city, those who had favored him, those who had sometimes fought him; but all of whom, men and women alike, had shared with him a deep faith in Atlanta's destiny.

The chronicle that follows is the story of how Bill Hartsfield strove to fulfill that destiny—and in so doing, left his mark on his town forever.

WILLIAM BERRY HARTSFIELD

THE TOWN THAT BORE HIM

By 1890, the year in which William B. Hartsfield was born, Atlanta had begun to march to a new song's measure. The bloody war that had brought Sherman and his incendiaries down upon the city was only a quarter century in the past, and it had not been forgotten. Jefferson Davis, the South's leader in that war, had only recently died, and Atlanta had deeply mourned for him. Gray veterans still walked the streets, nursing old battle scars, and the city had just built a refuge for the homeless among them, where they could sit and talk and dream of dangers past.

But Atlanta's eyes were on the future now. The mud and dust of its potholed, gaslit streets were beginning to give way to cobblestones and concrete; sewers were being laid, though houses served by the outdoor privy still outnumbered those with indoor plumbing three to one. Brick office buildings were going up in place of the wooden structures hastily erected after the war, and in the new houses rapidly rising on the outskirts of the town, the dim bulbs of the new electric light were replacing the gaslights or the smoky kerosene lamps of the 1880s. Most Atlantans still went about their business on foot or in buggies, carriages, or streetcars drawn by mules. But in April 1889 Joel Hurt's first electric streetcar had flowed smoothly out newly laid Edgewood Avenue to Inman Park. The snort and sputter of the gasoline automobile had not yet come to frighten the dray-horses drinking at the public water trough at Five Points. Life was stirring in all areas as the city moved into the decade of the nineties. The huge new state capitol had just been completed, Agnes Scott Institute had been founded, Georgia Tech graduated its first class, and Spelman College was sending into the world bright young black women splendidly trained in music and education. The first Elks Lodge was formed, and on Atlanta's street corners for the first time a Salvation Army band began to thump and tootle its invitation to the unsaved. And simmering in the back of several Atlantans' minds were plans for another great civic celebration—this one to embrace the world—the Cotton States and International Exposition.

It was in such an atmosphere of change, based on energy, vision, and high confidence, that William Berry Hartsfield, pet-named "Willie" by his parents, came bawling into the world. He was born in the house of his father, Charles Green Hartsfield, a tinsmith, at 44 North Butler Street. Butler Street, like the city, was then an unzoned mixture of residential and industrial structures old and new, and it is highly probable that the infant Hartsfield's birth-cries were drowned out by the screech and whine of the saws in the Phoenix Planing Mill across the street. A block to the north of the Hartsfield residence was the Atlanta Medical College, which during the war had served as a hospital where gray troops wounded in the fighting around Atlanta were brought to heal or die. And just beyond the Medical College, in December 1890, Masons with solemn ritual laid the cornerstone of Henry W. Grady Memorial Hospital. The great southern editor, orator, and triumphant visionary had died the year before, after a trip north to make his last, and one of his most prophetic speeches. In this address, to the Boston Merchants' Association, Grady uttered lines that foretold a future that only began to come to pass nearly ninety years later, with the election of a Georgian as President of the United States. He called on his friends in the North for loyalty to the republic of which all regions were a part. "This hour little needs the loyalty that is loyal to one section and yet holds the other in enduring suspicion and estrangement," he told a rapt audience. "Give us the broad and perfect loyalty that loves and trusts Georgia with Massachusetts, that knows no South, no North, no East, no West, but endows with equal and patriotic love every foot of our soil, every state in the Union."[1]

It was something of this broad and all encompassing love and understanding that Bill Hartsfield brought to his native city during his years in politics, as alderman, state legislator, and finally in nearly a quarter century as mayor. His concern was not primarily with a new and greater South, nor even a new and greater Georgia, but with a new and greater Atlanta. It was his firm belief that as Atlanta grew and prospered so would Georgia, and as Georgia thrived so would the South and the nation. Spending a lifetime struggling to fulfill this dream, he learned to know and understand every segment of the city's population and to love every foot of soil within its boundaries, which he strove constantly to expand.

Hartsfield had much of Grady's talent for persuading men of wealth and power to support his goals, and for more than two decades these men demonstrated in tangible ways their faith in him. But the tinsmith's son who was to find himself so much at home in the clubrooms and boardrooms of the mighty had in him too a strong streak of the populism that was making itself strongly felt in Georgia during his developing years. Although city-born and city-bred, he could comprehend the farmer's goals and problems. And within the boundaries of the city, he was at home in any company, and in most political races he could count on the trust and confidence of the Atlanta workingman. Equally important, in later years he was able to count on the support of Atlanta's black community, which would make up with its votes what he might sometimes lack in support from the white working class.

Hartsfield's knowledge of the Negro and of his aspirations was deeply rooted in his past. Not far from his house on Butler Street was the A.M.E. church, and beyond it there stretched north and east for blocks a black community. These youngsters were his childhood playmates in the easygoing camaraderie of the day. They roamed the streets together, and after heavy rains they prowled old battle areas, hunting the lead bullets that dealers bought at five cents a pound and melted down to make the soldering lead that sealed the pipes and gutters in the new houses that were springing up in Grant Park and Inman Park and out Peachtree and Washington streets. In Atlanta, as he grew up, ex-slaves and the children of slaves were beginning to create a new class of blacks, a well-to-do middle class whose members had broken at last the economic chains that had bound them, to become prosperous contractors, doctors, dentists, undertakers, insurance men, bankers, lawyers, and educators. Warren Cochran, John Wesley Dobbs, A. T. Walden, John Calhoun—to these men in later years Hartsfield would turn for help, and though they knew he had certain deep-seated prejudices in racial matters, they would send their people to the polls to vote for him. And this black support, plus the backing of the town's power structure, made him invulnerable until the political and social turmoil of the sixties shattered old voting patterns.

Where Hartsfield got the peculiar combination of talents that made him a preeminent figure among the nation's mayors is not immediately revealed by his genealogy. The Hartsfields were a doughty lot, landholders, soldiers, and men of mark in their community, but there seem to have been no politicians among them. It is believed that the clan originated in the Hartz mountains of Germany, where the family name was Hartzfelder. The first Hartsfield in America, though, was Andrew, a

Welshman who came to New York in 1726 and whose seed were later scattered through the South and Midwest. He had been a captain in the British Army, but once here, in any quarrel between colony and crown he took the patriot side. An acquisitive man, he soon owned some 160 acres of land in what is now the heart of Manhattan Island, comprising some of the most valuable real estate in the world. It remained in the family for two generations, when a grandson leased it to the city of New York for a period of ninety-nine years. There seems to have been some flaw in the transaction though, for the Hartsfield heirs were not able to recover title when the lease expired. Andrew of course was long since gone. He had left New York in 1733, to live for twenty-two years in Philadelphia; he then moved on to Wake County, North Carolina, where he died and was buried in 1759. The first Hartsfield in Georgia was his grandson, Richard. A private soldier in the Revolutionary War, he came to Oglethorpe County to take up lands there under grants from the state to soldiers who had fought against the crown. He begat Henry, who in turn sired Berry, the father of Charles, who became the father of William Berry Hartsfield. It is possible that it was from Berry Hartsfield's wife, Martha Jane Glenn, that William B. Hartsfield inherited some of his pluck and resolution. He was proud of recalling that his grandmother as a young girl had ridden horseback behind her father, holding to his waist, all the way from Virginia to Georgia.

Hartsfield's father, Charles, was eleven years old at the outbreak of the Civil War, and he saw his chance for formal schooling shattered by that conflict. Soon after it ended, he came to Atlanta to find work—and quickly discovered that the sack of Confederate money he had accepted from his brothers and sisters in payment for his share of the family lands was absolutely worthless.

Charles Hartsfield, a skilled tinsmith, worked with his hands all his life. He never received a formal education. To his son, though, there was a quality about him of the philosopher, of the teacher. Though he was quick to whack the rambunctious Willie across the bottom when he got out of hand, he preferred gentler measures. Sparing the rod, he would deliver a lecture worthy of a college professor on the proper behavior required of small boys. Though with the exception of Sundays he spent his life in work clothes, he insisted on dressing Willie in the height of the current fashion, including Fauntleroy coats and velvet breeches, and later, Buster Brown collars and flowing ties. A picture of Willie at age six shows him wearing a flowing black tie and a Buster Brown collar, standing in the front row of a large group of youngsters, proudly holding a slate proclaiming that this was "First Grade–A, Crew Street School, Atlanta, Ga., 1896." One of the older Hartsfield's rituals his son always remembered. At night after he and his older brothers John and Charles had gone to bed, their father would sit up by the fire, shining their shoes, then lining them up neatly under their beds. Once when he was small, young Hartsfield found beneath his Christmas stocking a little tin trunk, handcrafted by his father. To the boy it was a treasure, and he kept it all his years, taking it with him wherever he moved.

It was his mother though who had the greatest influence on his life, not only in his childhood but long into his mature years, when he was a husband and father and still living in her house. Once he had mused, idly, how he could tell who would make a good city employee and who would not. Throw a plank with a nail in it into the street, she told him. Then watch to see who passed it by—and who stopped to pick it up.

His father died in the flu epidemic of 1918. His mother lived eighteen years longer, dying in 1936—the year in which Hartsfield was first elected mayor. At his inauguration in 1937 admirers had much to say in praise of him. His reply was that he wished that his mother were alive to hear these things. She, he said, was the only one who would have believed them.

Willie, the youngest of three sons, was indeed his mother's favorite and he learned much from her that shaped his character. Victoria Dagnall Hartsfield herself was of sturdy pioneer stock. Her father, a Burke County farmer, had fought in the Mexican War and against the Seminoles in Florida; in the Civil War he had made rifles for the Confederacy at the armory in Augusta and salt at the refinery in Savannah. She was a young girl when Sherman's armies burned and pillaged their way through Georgia, and the sights and sounds of the war years remained vivid in her memory. Sitting by the fire at night, a cat asleep beside her chair, she sang to Willie the old songs of the Confederacy and told him stories of how she had been sent to the woods with a basket to hunt wild fruits and berries in those hungry days. Curiously she had no tendency to indulge in the Southern habit of describing the Yankee soldiers as fiends and devils. To her they were just like the Confederate troops—homesick youngsters yearning for the war to end. From her young Hartsfield learned two things. One, that the Southern cause was worthy of being remembered and dramatized in such tangible forms as the Cyclorama and the Stone Mountain Memorial carvings; and two, that he should treat all men fairly, white or black, rich or poor, Yankee or Southerner, remaining always understanding of their weaknesses and tolerant of their faults. It was a lesson that Hartsfield, a quick-tempered man, would often forget in the fierce political battles that were to come.

He responded early to the drama and excitement of politics, remembering in later years how boisterous sometimes drunken crowds would gather downtown on the night of a national election to see results brought in by Western Union flashed by lantern slides on sheets hung from the side of a building. He decided early, too, that although he greatly admired his father, he had no intention of spending his life working with his hands. (The memory of his father's fingers, eaten by the acids used in the tinsmith's trade, stayed with him for years.) Nor would he follow for long the modest white-collar pursuits of his older brothers, John, a stenographer, and Charles, a clerk.

In 1902 Charles Hartsfield, Sr., moved his family from the corner of Butler and Gilmer, now rapidly becoming an area of small shops and stores and populated by Atlantans whose names were Mediterranean in origin, to serene and quiet Milledge Avenue. Here, in the burgeoning Grant Park neighborhood, houses had front lawns and indoor plumbing. The lots were large, with room enough at back or side for a garden, or even room to keep a cow and a flock of chickens. From here he went to Boys High School, dropping out in his senior year to attend Dixie Business College at night, his tuition furnished by an aunt. He took a secretarial course, became extremely fast with his shorthand, and went to work as a stenographer for the American Radiator Company. He went from there to a clerk's job with the General Fire Extinguisher Company, where Robert Woodruff, a boyhood chum who shared Hartsfield's views on the value of a business career over formal education, was working as a salesman. When Woodruff moved on to become a buyer for the Atlantic Ice and Coal Company—which was expanding throughout the South in the early 1900s—Hartsfield wrote out, in a neat hand, the orders Woodruff had placed each day. The friendship that began between the two young men in their childhood lasted throughout their lives. Woodruff's faith in Hartsfield as an honest man of unshakable integrity never faltered as Hartsfield moved on into his political career; and Hartsfield never failed to turn to his friend Woodruff for counsel and support on all matters concerning the welfare of Atlanta. As Woodruff moved on with greater and greater success in the business world, from the Ice and Coal Company to the White Truck Company, and from there to the beginning of his fabulous career in the business of Coca-Cola, Hartsfield himself was moving ahead in a different field.

By 1913 he was prospering well enough in his clerkships to ask Pearl Williams for her hand in marriage. Miss Williams, an operator for the Western Union Telegraph Company, was four years older than Hartsfield. She was a gentle somewhat shy person, lacking Hartsfield's bounce and verve, and unable to share, perhaps even to understand, his fierce urge to make a name for himself. The courtship was sometimes stormy. Hartsfield was a jealous lover, and when he found out that Miss Williams had dated someone else, he would rebuke her sternly, using harsh language. Then he would go home and write a deeply contrite letter of apology. Soon after their marriage Hartsfield's oldest brother, John, a stenographer and clerk, died at the family home on Milledge Avenue at the age of thirty-four. John's death may have discouraged Hartsfield from following in his brother's footsteps as a clerk and contributed to his feeling that life in a more prestigious profession would offer greater rewards. This decision was a turning point. In 1916 he went to work as a clerk, while at the same time reading law, in the prestigious legal firm of Rosser, Slaton, Phillips and Hopkins. Luther Rosser was a legendary figure in Georgia legal circles and John Slaton was a Georgia governor who gained national renown for his high courage when in 1915 he commuted the death sentence of Leo Frank. Association with men of the calibre of these law partners soon taught Hartsfield that if he were to travel in the same intellectual circles, he must learn far more than he had been taught in high school and business school. But for a man with a wife to support—and soon a son and daughter as well—going to college was out of the question. His solution was simple; he would educate himself, in the humanities and in the law. He wrote to the deans of a half dozen of the more prestigious colleges, told them he had foolishly dropped out of high school, and asked them for a list of books that would give him a well-rounded education. The suggestions poured in, and from then on, night after night for a period of several years,

Hartsfield spent his evenings poring over a book in the public library. He became familiar with the poets, the dramatists, the historians, the philosophers, the humanists, and in after years his speeches were laced with erudite references, dramatic lines, and gentle humor. He was equally at ease welcoming a black-tie audience to the symphony, addressing a business group, or greeting an assembly of scientists. Geology particularly fascinated him, and he kept a lifelong interest in developing Georgia's mineral resources. He was proud of the fact he was self-educated and would boast that the Atlanta Public Library was his alma mater.

In the law office by day, between his clerkly duties, he would read insatiably in the law books that surrounded him, and in later years he said he probably was the only man in history who, by his own choice, had read Blackstone twice. He found it boring; but boring or not, in 1917 he passed the Georgia Bar exam—a proud moment for all his family.

Another event in 1917, which would shape his life thereafter, was not so glorious and unhappily would create enduring tensions between him and his wife and children. After his marriage in 1913 he and Pearl had set up housekeeping, first on Washington Street, then on Courtland, then on Boulevard Terrace, where their first child, William Berry Hartsfield, Jr., was born. They had hardly settled in at this last address when, on the morning of May 21, 1917, the great Atlanta fire broke out. They got out safely, with a few possessions, but their house was burned along with all the other houses on that pleasant little street. Many Atlantans slept in the streets that night, their homes and all their possessions destroyed. The Hartsfields were luckier; they moved into his parents' house on Milledge Avenue. There they were happily welcomed and there they remained for the next twenty-seven years. They probably would have soon moved on to another house of their own, but in the year following the fire Charles Green Hartsfield died at the age of sixty-nine, and in 1919 Pearl gave birth to a daughter, Mildred. To Hartsfield it was logical for him and his family to stay on, sparing his widowed mother the pangs of living with only her bachelor son, Charles, to keep her company. And with his mother there, his wife would have the benefit of her advice on childrearing and on the art of feeding, comforting, and pleasing a husband. There is some reason to believe that the old aphorism that no house is big enough for a mother and her daughter-in-law was applicable in this case. Whatever reservations Pearl Hartsfield might have felt, there is no doubt that from her husband's standpoint it was an ideal arrangement. So here began the life-style he would follow as political ambition began to stir in him. He would work hard in his office by day. By night he would roam the city to which in his heart he was married and whose electorate in time would become his only true family.

GONE WITH THE WIND —
HIS PROUDEST MOMENT

BILL HARTSFIELD's love affair with his city began early. One sunny afternoon in 1909, a skinny young high-school dropout with a few hours to kill, he rode out to a grassy field near Hapeville, on the outskirts of Atlanta. His mission was to watch the newfangled racing cars thundering and sputtering around a dusty oval known as the Candler racetrack. He went home to Milledge Avenue wide-eyed with excitement. It was not the roaring automobiles, kicking up their plumes of dust, that had impressed him. It was the clean, by comparison almost quiet, flight of a little monoplane, flown by a Frenchman named Moisant, that swooped low, bobbing and weaving, above the center field of the racetrack.

It was the first airplane that Hartsfield had ever seen, and the first of thousands of planes that in years to come would land and take off at this place that was first to be known as Candler Field, later as Atlanta Municipal Airport, and finally as Hartsfield International. At every step of its progress Bill Hartsfield was its patron saint. In 1923, two years after he had gone into the private practice of law, he ran for and won his first political race—for alderman from the Third Ward. Still skinny and jug-eared, but amazingly self-assured, he was immediately made chairman of the new aviation committee of city council. In the fourteen years that had passed since the wide-eyed youngster had watched the Frenchman tool his little monoplane up and down the racetrack, the Candler Speedway, though still an auto-racing center, had seen more and more aircraft come in. During World War I army fliers in helmets and goggles had flown their stubwinged biplanes into Atlanta, sponsoring Liberty Bond drives. After the war barnstormers and wing-walkers had made the Candler Speedway their center of operations. Two of them, Beeler Blevins and Doug Davis, were flying from there, taking people over town on Saturday for five dollars a head.

Soon they were flying Alderman Hartsfield on a special mission. Asa Candler, owner of the three-hundred-acre racetrack, had offered the city a five-year lease on the land if the city would pay the county taxes on it. The idea was that at the end of that time the city would buy the land outright if a price could be agreed on. Mayor Walter Sims asked Hartsfield to check into the proposal and make his recommendations, for there were others eager to sell their land to the city. Week after week, with Blevins or Davis, or a pilot named George Shealey at the controls, Hartsfield flew over every area of open land around Atlanta. He even learned to fly a plane himself so that he could look at the terrain through a pilot's eyes. (He flew as pilot once and never took the controls thereafter.) On weekends he would take his son, William Jr., and his little daughter, Mildred, aged nine and six, on long and, to them, seemingly meaningless and rambling drives. He was checking out, from the ground, areas he had looked at from the air. Fellow councilmen had a financial interest in some of these sites, and they brought pressure to bear on him; but nothing he looked at seemed more suitable than the Candler property. It was high, dry, reasonably level, without swamps and meadows, and had plenty of open land around it. It also had some citizens around it who felt that an airfield would be a vast annoyance. One man said the planes frightened his cows, causing them to drop their calves too soon and to quit giving milk. Well, said Hartsfield, how much did he want for his pasture? A thousand dollars, the man said. The city bought his land, and a few years later sold a portion of it for $400,000. A great many people argued, with great vehemence, that no city had the right to spend taxpayers' money on airfields that would be used mainly by rich sportsmen and young maniacs determined to break their necks. Hartsfield soothed them. The city was not spending any money for the first five years, he pointed out, for the county had been persuaded to forego taxes on the land. In 1929, at Hartsfield's urging, the city bought the leased land, paying $94,000 for 297 acres. And so the groundwork was laid for the great air terminal that, like the railroads of the 1840s, assured Atlanta's entry into the modern age. There had been some elements involved, of course, other than the purchase of land. When the first airways to be lighted by flashing beacons were planned by federal aviation authorities, Birmingham, not Atlanta, was to be a terminal and transfer point on the routes between New York and Miami and between Jacksonville and Chicago. This decision outraged Hartsfield, who persuaded the city's business leaders to invite the federal official responsible for these routings to come to Atlanta. He was met at the railroad station by a motorcycle escort, which led him through town to an elaborate dinner where the city's top businessmen, plus the mayor and the governor, treated him to honors that would have satisfied an oriental potentate's desire for pomp and circumstance. Atlanta got the air route, and it was years before Birmingham realized that Hartsfield had in effect hijacked their air terminal.

Hartsfield was particularly adept at putting his city's best foot forward—as well as his own. In 1927 when Charles Lindbergh came to town, all the city's bigwigs turned out to greet him at the airfield. Hartsfield, being merely an alderman, was not among the official welcoming group. He made sure though that his presence did not go unnoticed. He rode as escort, just behind the motorcycles, in an open car with Fire Chief William B. Cody, waving jovially to the throngs that had gathered to see Lindbergh.

Hartsfield in the early days of the airport's operation acted as a self-appointed manager and security guard. He would go out on Saturdays and Sundays to help keep the crowds in order, for it was hard to tell runways from parking areas and excited motorists sometimes drove in front of taxiing planes. Not long after the lighted air route was completed, the airmail came in, and in 1927 a young company called Pitcairn Aviation, Incorporated (soon to be reorganized as Eastern Airlines) built the first hangars at Candler Field. The city put up a two-story building for eight thousand dollars, and at Hartsfield's urging offered it to the federal aviation officials rent free. Hartsfield's enthusiasm for promoting Atlanta as an aviation center rubbed off on hotelman Carling Dinkler, who offered a free bed for the night to any visitor from another city coming into Atlanta by air.

Night flying began in 1927, and Hartsfield was determined that Atlanta should become an around-the-clock airport. With the city electrician, he traveled all over the East and Midwest, looking at the lighting systems at other airfields. Finding nothing he considered worthy of Atlanta, he finally decided to create his own. He chose a huge curved lens, developed in Holland and sold in this country by General Electric. Soon delegates from other cities were coming to Atlanta to look at Candler Field's lights. In recognition of his labors for the airport, the Chamber of Commerce in 1928 awarded Hartsfield its Certificate of Distinguished Achievement.

In that year he returned briefly to the private practice of law —and to certain other matters that had begun to interest him. Somewhere in his omnivorous self-imposed reading, he had picked up a knowledge of geology that was almost professional in its scope. His main interest was in the talcs and clays, shales and aggregates of Georgia, and even in lean times he somehow found money to invest in mining operations. His interest in the earth's treasures led him to oil exploration and to the financing of wildcat drilling operations in other states. He made very little money in any of these private ventures, and in some of them he lost his shirt, but his interest in them never flagged.

Hartsfield in 1927 had made the acquaintance of a man as much addicted to ground transport by motor vehicle as Hartsfield was a believer in traveling the ocean of air. Young John Steinmetz came to Atlanta from Saint Paul, Minnesota, in the mid-twenties, bringing with him the idea that he could develop a network of motor-coach and truck lines that would put trains and streetcars out of business. Hartsfield acted as Steinmetz's lawyer while Steinmetz, backed by midwestern businessmen, began buying up short-haul jitney bus lines that were running in all directions out of Atlanta. His first line ran from Atlanta to Macon in 1927 and later was followed by routes to Columbus and to Augusta by way of Athens and Monroe. He moved west next, toward Carrollton, pushing for Birmingham. Finally, with Hartsfield's quiet help in buying up the needed franchises, Steinmetz's Dixie Safety Coach Company was operating from Miami to Chicago, Augusta to New York, and from Atlanta to Birmingham and Montgomery.

Jean Martin, writing of Steinmetz and Hartsfield in his book *Mule to Marta*,[1] is convinced that the long bus rides they took together first planted in Hartsfield's mind the deep belief in highway transportation that later led to his strong support of the interstate expressway system, as well as the metropolitan rapid transit concept out of which evolved MARTA. He also shared Steinmetz's conviction that motor buses were cheaper and more efficient carriers than electric streetcars and trackless trolleys. So convinced was he, in fact, that in 1932 and 1933 he and Steinmetz tried to buy the electric streetcar lines in Rome, Georgia, Anniston, Alabama, and Columbia, South Carolina with the idea of replacing them with bus lines. The power companies would have been happy to sell but were prevented by state laws that would not permit separation of the street railways.

In 1933 he ran for the state legislature from Fulton County, won, and found himself going back to his first love, the airplane and the promotion of Atlanta as a great regional air terminal. Remembering the trouble protesting citizens had caused him when he tried to buy the Candler land for the city, his first act in the House was to introduce a bill that would authorize a city or a county, or a combination of the two, to build and operate airports whose facilities would be rented to airline operators and concessionaires.

Though Hartsfield was a representative of Fulton County in the General Assembly, the group that was still closest to his heart was the great human family of Atlanta. And when he felt that his fellow legislators were not being as sympathetic as they should to Atlanta's special needs he would sometimes explode in a fit of rage that would bring the reporters scurrying from the pressroom. On one occasion, making a point, he banged his fist so fiercely down on the rail before the speaker's desk that he broke his hand. Another time, seeking the floor, he stormed down the aisle bellowing "Mister Speakah, Mister Speakah," and climbed up on the clerk's desk to confront Speaker E. D. Rivers nose to nose.

Thus began the volatile personal style that was to become typical of Hartsfield in all his years in politics. He had an unerring instinct for backing measures that were to prove wise and just—and an equally infallible capacity for infuriating a great number of people in the process. After the campaigns that put him in the legislature for two terms, Hartsfield was never again a wide-eyed innocent in politics. In his second race, in 1934, his opponent, P. C. McDuffie, distinguished Atlanta real estate developer, denounced Hartsfield as a tool of the Fulton County "ring." This nefarious political clique, McDuffie claimed, was made up in large degree of the judges and attendants of the municipal court (whose chief judge was Luther Z. Rosser, in whose father's office Hartsfield had read law). It was this group, said McDuffie, who were "hauling Hartsfield over the county in county-owned cars . . . at the expense of suffering taxpayers, in a desperate effort to stem the tide that is carrying their political agent out to oblivion."[2]

The tide instead swept Hartsfield back into office for another term. At the end of this second term he was ready to make his move for the office he really wanted. In 1936 he ran against the aging James L. Key for the office of mayor and found himself subjected to political abuse that made all the imprecations he had endured before seem like the gentle cooing of a flock of doves. Key was a veteran of the political wars and a master of political invective and damaging innuendo. First in letters, then from the stump, he charged Hartsfield with trying to bribe a city councilman, with offering to get another lawyer's client out of the stockade if, in turn, this lawyer would split his fees with him; and of starting an amusements company that quickly went bankrupt, causing several Atlanta business concerns to lose their money. He also charged that Hartsfield owed his doctor eighty-six dollars on a bill that had been outstanding for four years.

By now Hartsfield himself was a master at heaping political contumely on the head of an opponent, while ignoring or passing off lightly the charges against himself. If all the people who owed a doctor bill voted for him, he said, he would be a shoo-in. He then turned the discussion to certain flaws in Mayor Key's character. The police department under Mayor Key, he said, was demoralized, the officers not knowing whose arrest might cost them their jobs. Bootleggers, he said, moved freely about the police station, and there was reason to believe that some of the higher officials drank to excess. Bellowing from the back of a secondhand sound-truck lit by flares, Hartsfield charged that Key, by pardoning a prominent attorney charged with a traffic violation and by refusing to demand the resignation of a member of his police committee who was arrested for drunkenness, had failed to back up his own men. He was particularly scathing in his attack on Key for an alleged insult to the Confederacy. "Never before has Atlanta had a mayor who was mean enough and had gall enough to veto a resolution establishing Memorial Day in Atlanta as a holiday, but Key did just that."[3] Hartsfield also faulted the mayor for spending only an hour a day at City Hall and for allowing a new jail to be constructed so shoddily that "criminals carved their way out singly and in droves with pocket knives."[4] Hartsfield also concentrated his fire on Key's two top cops, Chief T. O. Sturdivant, head of the uniformed force, and A. Lamar Poole, chief of detectives, promising to fire them both if he was elected.

Atlantans seemed unimpressed by what Key and Hartsfield said about each other, though in the primary they favored Hartsfield by a whisker—8,951 votes to 8,534 for Key. A third candidate, businessman James L. Wells, got 3,073 votes. In the runoff between Hartsfield and Key, Hartsfield's message seemed to get across, for he picked up all of Wells's votes, a handful of Key's, and won easily, 12,348 to 8,174.

Deeply moved, he addressed the voters, thanking them for their support. His wife and children shared his triumph, but in this moment his thoughts turned to his mother who had died at the age of eighty-three earlier in the year. "If there were but one thing in the world I could have now, it would be to have my dear mother, who passed away last February, with me. She was always my inspiration and chief supporter in my former races for alderman and member of the legislature. When I take office as mayor, the first thing I am going to do is place her picture on my desk, and I know I can look there and find the right answer to many of the perplexing problems that are ahead of me."[5]

There were several others to whom Hartsfield might have paid his private thanks. In the weeks before he announced his candidacy for mayor, he had borrowed all he could on his insurance and still had had some doubts that he would be able to finance the race. His friend John Steinmetz assured him that he could count on help from many friends. Hartsfield seemed dubious and Steinmetz decided to show him. He left, promising to be back in two hours with some money. He had a cup of coffee, walked around a while, went to his own bank and drew out roughly five hundred dollars in small bills, and went back to Hartsfield's office. There he started pulling money from all his pockets and piling it on Hartsfield's desk, indicating that he had called on a number of Atlantans with a great deal of success. Hartsfield immediately made him his official fund raiser.

Another friend who smoothed Hartsfield's path was Robert Woodruff. In December 1936, just before Hartsfield took office in January, Woodruff held out a helping hand to the city. In the grim depression years the city paid its employees in scrip, which most merchants and banks had been cashing at a heavy discount. Woodruff, at Hartsfield's request, let it be known that The Coca-Cola Company would absorb the full amount of the December payroll issue, some $730,000 going to four thousand city employees, many of whom were schoolteachers. Naturally with Coca-Cola in effect guaranteeing the city's promise-to-pay, banks and merchants immediately started to cash the scrip at face value. It was indeed, as a *Constitution* editorial pointed out, a generous response to the city's needs and a fine gesture of higher citizenship on the part of Woodruff and his company.

The city, as Hartsfield first took office as mayor, was in poor financial shape, and in his inaugural address to city council on

January 4, 1937, he clearly outlined the problems they all faced. The city, he said, was thirteen million dollars in debt. It was giving away, to some favored citizens, city services for which payment should be received. Neither general council nor any of its committees had the responsibility for administering the city departments; this was the job of the department heads, and he required them to start at once to operate their departments more economically and efficiently. They should begin by firing unneeded employees and by making an intelligent revision of haphazard salary scales. The county, he said, should be asked to take on a fairer share of the burden of government services that benefit both city and county residents—streets, hospitals, and the administration of relief. Atlanta, he said, spent more on relief than any city of its size in the nation. The sale of wine and beer was legal, if properly licensed, but the licensing system had been haphazard and many of the places where wine and beer were sold had turned into dives and joints where anybody, of any age, could buy any kind of alcohol they wanted. He recommended that license fees be raised, license laws be strictly enforced, and all sales of wine and beer be forbidden on Sunday. Another shameful aspect of the city's operation was traffic control. "Our downtown streets are jammed and the slaughter of our people has reached shameful proportions . . . Traffic is a matter to be handled as a scientific and engineering problem, without political considerations and coupled with rigid enforcement," Hartsfield insisted. This brought him to his favorite campaign target—the police department. One thing he said in which the people of Atlanta were in complete agreement was the need to give the police department an "immediate, impartial, fearless, and complete overhauling." The department, once it had been purged of its dishonest and inefficient members, should be turned over to the best leader that could be found, and that person should fairly and impartially enforce the law without interference. Once this was done, he said, "hundreds of criminal characters and law violators who now infest our city may find it to their interest to bid us farewell forever."

Looking ahead, he recommended that the police department, the fire department, and traffic control be brought under a new director of public safety, to be authorized by the legislature and appointed by the mayor—a man of outstanding administrative ability, who would appoint his own chiefs who in turn would appoint their own officers, whom they could promote or demote to the ranks at will. The director of public safety would also have the responsibility of studying the future and laying out plans to meet the needs of a growing city.

The new mayor then closed on the note of challenge and of confidence that would be typical of his public utterances in the years to come:

You and I may as well face the fact that our people now demand of us a right-about-face in the conduct of this government, and will stand for no petty strife or selfish political manipulation. I take office with a feeling of humble gratefulness to the people of Atlanta [and] without the slightest thought of political favoritism or ill will toward a single member of the great human family of Atlanta. I ask of you and each department head and every employee only the efficient and honest performance of their duties. The problems we face are not insurmountable. As long as we are not under an impossible bonded indebtedness and the real resources of our great and growing city are still intact, and there is a clear majority of honest, law abiding and patriotic citizens who will support the advocates of good government, these problems can and will be solved.

The about-face he had promised began at once. The day after his inauguration Police Chief T. O. Sturdivant and Chief of Detectives A. Lamar Poole turned in their badges, and Harts-field named a veteran police lieutenant, Marion A. Hornsby, as chief of police. Immediately a strong campaign was launched against gamblers and racketeers, particularly against the "bug," a lottery operation. By March outraged bugmen were sending

Hartsfield anonymous threats, and Hornsby thought it advisable to give him a bodyguard. There was no letup in the city's attack on malefactors, and by September most of the more lurid hot spots in town had been closed. Fulton County cooperated by initiating a grand-jury investigation of graft and organized crime. Police roaring through town in pursuit of speeders or suspected bug pickup men brought strong protests from some law-abiding citizens, who claimed their lives were being endangered. Such protests resulted in the use of hidden police, who popped out of a side street to overtake a speeder before he could make a run for it. This tactic, however, was politically damaging to Hartsfield. Some citizens were caught a dozen times or more, trundling along at thirty in a twenty-five-mile-an-hour zone, and the impression soon was widespread that these arrests were actually revenue measures, a form of tax on the motorist.

Atlanta was teetering on the brink of bankruptcy as Hartsfield took over, and indeed his first and most pressing concern was the city's financial condition. The city had been operating on an outdated system of budgeting that allowed it to spend on a basis of anticipated revenues, a hit-or-miss plan that created an ever-increasing deficit. Soon, though, the word was out in financial circles that Robert Woodruff had full confidence in the honesty, character, and financial ability of Bill Hartsfield, and thus reassured, the banks willingly helped the new mayor refinance the more pressing obligations.

The legislature then took the most important step. At Hartsfield's urging it passed legislation setting up a model budget system for the city which provided that no department could budget more than 99 percent of the money it had actually received in the previous year. To provide a margin for safety, the council usually limited the budget to 95 percent of the previous year's receipts. The system has worked remarkably well ever since. The city frequently ends the year with a substantial cash carry-over. No money is borrowed for operating purposes, and when bonds are sold to build expressways, schools, parks, airfields, libraries, sewers, and other capital improvements, they sell at a premium.

Hartsfield was also pleased, as he looked back over his first year in office, that his department heads had eliminated 165 unneeded positions, and that his new chief of police, Hornsby, had weeded out several persons in the department who were suspected of being in cahoots with gangsters. There were still plenty of undesirable characters around who had a financial interest in law violation, Hartsfield told the city council as he began his second year in office, but he remained adamant in his determination that they should be run out of town.

The city in 1938 was gradually beginning to throw off the shackles of depression, but more revenue was desperately needed if it was to improve its services. One possible source of revenue, Hartsfield suggested, was Fulton County, which he felt was still not paying its full share for services—such as Grady Hospital, Battle Hill Sanitarium, Carnegie Library, the municipal airport, and police and fire protection for certain areas— that the city provided to residents of city and county alike. The airport was still much on his mind, since he was the father of it. Some way, he insisted, must be found to improve the traffic control tower and to extend the runways. If this vital part of Atlanta's transportation facilities was neglected, the city's growth could not continue.

With the city's finances straightened out and its police department reorganized and working smoothly—his two main concerns when he took office—Hartsfield turned to another idea which he would promote with great zeal throughout his years as mayor—the development of Atlanta as a great tourist center. His mother's stories of the Civil War, his boyhood spent prowling old battle lines, hunting for relics, had left him with the conviction that Atlanta's history was one of its treasured resources. The Cyclorama, he felt, should draw thousands of visitors to Atlanta, and Stone Mountain was an awe-inspiring geological relic that could easily be made into a fabulous tourist attraction. His dream encompassed the whole area where the Blue and Gray had fought, and since it had been a war between brothers, he looked for the day when the federal government would mark and landscape the old battlefields and maintain them as a national park. Hartsfield, for all his hard-nosed determination that his city should be a place of business and industry, was also as determined that it should be a place of beauty, with quiet little parks tucked away between the tall buildings, where people could sit and rest and look at grass and flowers and listen to the falling waters of a fountain. In 1938 he placed before council a proposal to create such an oasis in the form of a triangular park in front of the municipal auditorium. It took two years to bring about, but on November 23, 1940 Joel Hurt Park was dedicated and an electric fountain, given to the city by the Emily and Ernest Woodruff Foundation, began to play. It was the first new park in the downtown area since the Civil War, and Hartsfield had to fight hard to get it, over the opposition of downtown Atlanta real estate developers, notably Ben Massell, who thought a plaza over the railroad gulch should be devoted to business structures. Hurt Park therefore was actually a compromise. Hartsfield had wanted an open mall running all the way through from the terminal station to the auditorium.[6]

While beautifying the inner city, Hartsfield also worked incessantly throughout his long career to push the city limits further and further outward. The migration to the suburbs of Atlanta's best business and professional people alarmed and angered him, for this meant that the inner city would be dominated by the labor vote, which occasionally showed distressing signs of favoring his opponents Charlie Brown and Roy LeCraw. He was determined to recapture by annexation those in

the Buckhead area, where a number of the well-to-do had concentrated. He moved first to bring in those living in the area
from Palisades Road northward to Wesley Road, a feat that
took more than ten years to accomplish. It was one of the few
projects to which he set his mind that he could not push through
in a hurry. He took his troubles philosophically, however, once
telling a "Woman of the Year" audience, "I have learned that
to be a good mayor you must follow three principles: first, don't
take yourself too seriously; two, don't bite off more than you
can chew; and three, *don't bother Buckhead*." [7]

While pushing to bring in households from beyond the city
limits, he was curiously reluctant, at first, for the city to create
its own Public Housing Authority which would administer slum
clearance and rebuilding projects within the city. Atlantan
Charles F. (Chuck) Palmer, a real-estate man turned public-
housing zealot, had worked with his friend Eleanor Roosevelt,
to create the first federal housing project, Techwood Homes,
which replaced a fetid slum in the shadow of Georgia Tech.
Dedicated in 1935, this was the first such project in the United
States, and it was soon followed by University Homes for Negroes. Mayor Hartsfield was curiously disinclined to go beyond
this, though, until he was assured that the federal government
would continue to bear 90 percent of the building costs.

Hartsfield in his first term as mayor discovered that he had a
particular flair for ceremony, for welcoming visitors, whatever
their mission, in ways they would not soon forget. In January
1939 he greeted high prelates of the Catholic church, come to
dedicate the Co-Cathedral of Christ the King, and with Governor Rivers he sat among the special guests. On July 17 he
welcomed Dr. George W. Truett, president of the Baptist World
Alliance, which in the fortnight following brought thousands of
Baptists from many countries to a tremendous evangelistic assembly that packed Ponce de Leon Park. In November the
three Methodist denominations in Georgia came together at last

to heal the wounds caused by the slavery issue nearly a hundred years before.

In all these gatherings Hartsfield played the genial representative of the host city. In his next, and most triumphant public appearance, though, he helped shape the great event and played a starring role. By the spring of 1936 Margaret Mitchell's great novel, *Gone with the Wind,* just published, had begun its spectacular rise to fame, and David O. Selznick had bought the movie rights for fifty thousand dollars. Almost immediately reports, unsupported by any firm fact, began to circulate in Atlanta that the premiere of the picture would be held there, though no date was given. What this would mean to Atlanta was not lost on Mayor Hartsfield, who immediately began to lay his plans for making this an earthshaking event. (There was reason to suspect that it was he who had planted the rumor in the first place.) Nor did the prospect fail to interest certain ladies of the Junior League, whose roots went deep into old Atlanta. Mrs. William A. Parker, Mrs. Malon C. Courts, Mrs. Green Warren, and Mrs. Joseph Cooper called on Margaret Mitchell to get her approval of a great *Gone with the Wind* Ball, to be sponsored by the league in support of their charities, and to be held the night before the premiere.

And so, quietly through the spring and into the summer, they laid their plans. And then in mid-July the heavens fell. An official of Metro-Goldwyn-Mayer, which was to distribute the picture, passing through from Miami, dropped the dreadful word that the studio was planning to hold the premiere in New York.

A letter from Margaret Mitchell to Mrs. Allen Taylor, in New Jersey, reported what happened when the ladies of the Junior League heard the devastating news. "The ladies descended on Mayor Hartsfield's office like a pack of well-dressed Eumenides. His Honor, a passionate Confederate and a stout defender of Atlanta's civic rights and honors, leapt eight feet in the air when the ladies told him the rumor . . . Mayor Hartsfield announced to the Press that this was the worst outrage since Sherman burned the town. Of course, Atlanta was going to have the premiere, said the Mayor, 'for in a large way the book belongs to all of us.' "[8]

No sooner had the ladies left than Hartsfield fired off telegrams of protest to Selznick and to William R. Ferguson of MGM. Selznick's reply was prompt and reassuring. The rumors that Mr. Hartsfield had heard had no foundation, he said. Neither his company, nor Loew's, Incorporated, the distributor of the picture, had ever given any thought to an opening in any place but Atlanta.

Much relieved, Hartsfield gathered a great bouquet of magnolia blossoms, which he sent to Wilbur Kurtz, who was working on the picture, for delivery to Selznick in Culver City. He followed up with a letter assuring Selznick that Atlanta was determined to make this world premiere the greatest single outstanding event of its kind in the history of the cinema and telling him of the Junior League's plans for a great costume ball. He then urged that Selznick send all the principals of the cast to Atlanta to be presented at the ball—and if there were any props or costumes used in the picture lying about, "it would certainly be a wonderful gesture of mutual publicity value for a few of them to be sent to Atlanta."[9]

Evidently Selznick thought so too, for soon word reached Atlanta that the studio was sending a Confederate general's uniform, a Confederate private's uniform, a dress of Scarlett's with a red taffeta skirt and an eggshell chiffon waist, and the dress Melanie wore to the party when Ashley Wilkes came home from the war. Rich's was having mannequins made to fit these costumes, and after the premiere they would be put on permanent display at the Cyclorama.

Even so, Hartsfield and Atlanta waited nervously through the late summer and early fall of 1939, for the date of the showing had not yet been set. Finally on November 4 came a telegram from Howard Dietz of MGM. *Gone with the Wind* would have its world premiere at Loew's Grand Theater on Friday, December 15, at 8:15 P.M. Hartsfield's joy was boundless. He immediately notified *Life Magazine,* urging them to start making their plans to cover it. He sent out special invitations to mayors of all the surrounding southern states, and he had beautifully printed invitations sent out by the thousands. Under the crossed flags of the Confederacy, with the message "Furled but not Forgotten," and over the signature of William B. Hartsfield, Mayor, the invitation read, "The City Government and the people of Atlanta welcome you to the *Gone with the Wind* Celebration and World Premiere." Hartsfield turned out to be the picture's most effective promoter. In an address over WSB he promised his radio audience that Atlanta's premiere would be the greatest event of its kind in the entire world —an event that in its brilliance and nationwide interest would eclipse anything else ever attempted in the country before. He went on to describe the ball that would follow the premiere, a gala affair that would make all previous Atlanta social events pale into insignificance. Then he reassured those who might feel that they were out of place at such a glittering assembly. "We are going to make arrangements to see that everybody has a good time—Judy O'Grady and the Colonel's lady—the man in the limousine and the man on the street." [10]

The actual event exceeded Hartsfield's fondest hopes. Of the premiere, an awestruck journalist wrote:

Choked by emotions too deep for tears Atlanta watched Friday night as at last upon the screen of Loew's Grand the storm wind blew until an empire fell and its broken fragments tumbled before the hurricane into the mists of time. Men and women who had not understood quite rightly what the old folks meant when they told in trembling voices their passionate stories knew at last what their grandfathers fought for, what their grandmothers suffered for— and what mingled streams of gallantry and folly and courage blend in their own blood today. [11]

The great ball was, as Hartsfield promised, the most spectacular event of its kind ever seen in Atlanta. The Hollywood stars
began arriving in Atlanta on December 13. First to arrive was
Vivian Leigh, who, seated between Mayor Hartsfield and David O. Selznick, was whisked from the airport to the Georgian
Terrace Hotel. Gable arrived late the next afternoon in time to
join the great parade down Forsyth and Whitehall streets. By
this time, reports historian Franklin Garrett, the city was in a
frenzy of excitement, and there were more people packed along
the line of march than there were in the combined armies of
Sherman and Hood during the battle of Atlanta in 1864. A
brilliantly lighted platform had been put up at the corner of
Peachtree and Ponce de Leon, and as the guests arrived there
they left their automobiles and mounted the platform, where
Mayor Hartsfield introduced them. First he presented E. D.
Rivers, governor of Georgia, who in turn introduced his fellow
southern governors. Then Hartsfield took over again to present
to the cheering thousands each one of the actors in the picture.

That night, in an auditorium draped with Confederate flags,
smilax, and laurel, Atlantans reveled in their past, listening
teary-eyed to Enrico Leide's special arrangements of "Suwanee
River," "My Old Kentucky Home," and "Carry Me Back to Old
Virginny." They danced to waltzes, cheered the rousing war
songs, and beamed joyfully upon each other. The next morning
in the *Atlanta Georgian* a huge picture of the throng bore an
irreverent but affectionate caption by picture editor Tom Ham:
"They draped the hall for Auld Lang Syne, with Flags of Stars
and Bars, and all the Local Belles were there, and All their Ma's
and Pa's." Major Clark Howell, epitome of the old Atlanta, was
master of ceremonies, dressed in the costume of Dr. Meade in
the movie. He introduced the choir of the Ebenezer Baptist
Church, which was singing spirituals, and then the celebrities
were presented, one by one, ending with Gable, whom he introduced in the Junior League manner, says Garrett, as Mr. Carole

Lombard. During an interval, Mayor Hartsfield joined with Mrs. Colquitt Carter and Governor Rivers in an NBC radio broadcast that carried their description of the festivities to a national audience.

The premiere on the next night, when 2,031 of Atlanta's Four Hundred packed Loew's Grand to see what they fondly believed to be the world of their ancestors brought to the screen in living color, was equally spectacular. Blazing spotlights swept across the columned Tara facade built upon the old theater, as Julian Boehm introduced each arriving star to the cheering thousands packed in the streets in front of the theater. Once inside, the Hollywood visitors sat in their boxes, to be introduced again, one by one, as the filmed introduction rolled and their names and faces flashed upon the screen. (Hartsfield, who with his daughter Mildred sat in the box with Clark Gable and Carole Lombard, suffered an embarrassing accident as the crowd thronged in. The white tie of his full-dress suit lost its clasp, and he faced the prospect of confronting the great throng with his Adam's apple exposed. Gable saved the day, sending a messenger racing to his suite at the Georgian Terrace to bring back an extra tie for the Mayor.)

Willard Cope, reporter for the *Constitution,* summed up the events of the evening in the paper the next morning. "It was Hollywood, but it was also Atlanta. It was theater, but also life."[12] It was also Bill Hartsfield, and those who had come from Hollywood were sincere in their praise of what he had done. From Selznick came a long telegram in which he praised the Atlanta police force for its protection of the stars and asked particularly about a policeman who had been injured. "My Dear Mayor Hartsfield," said Selznick, "I cannot adequately express my appreciation for the wonderful way in which we were treated in Atlanta and for the extremes to which you personally went to make our trip a happy and successful one. So long as we live none of us will ever forget the days we spent there."

Later a short letter came from him to Hartsfield. "Mrs. Selz-nick and I have just unpacked the set of dishes which we brought from Atlanta and realized more than ever its beauty. We appreciate more than ever this permanent evidence of the kindliness with which we were received in Atlanta, and want to give you once more our earnest thanks."

Carole and Clark Gable wrote a cordial thank-you note for a reel of film Hartsfield had taken at the premiere and the ball. "We want to tell you how grateful we are for your kindness in making it for us. We ran it immediately and a very strange feeling came over us. It made us very homesick for you all, and again impressed upon our memory what a great event it was in our lives. As I said to Mr. Gable last night it will be so wonder-ful to look back on in the years to come. One of the most pleas-ant things about our trip was meeting and knowing you, as you were one of the main highlights."[13]

There were other highlights ahead. Still glowing from the success of the *Gone with the Wind* premiere, Hartsfield sat up far into the night at City Hall, signing checks for more than eight hundred thousand dollars, which paid all the city's bills for 1939—and still left a half million dollars in the bank. And in November 1940 the beautiful little Hurt Park for which he had fought so bitterly was at last dedicated.

But by now his political luck had run out. Made overconfi-dent by the ease with which he had cleared up the city's fi-nances, cleaned up its police force, beautified it with parks, and brought worldwide attention to its wonders through the *Gone with the Wind* premiere, he did not campaign with the fierce fervor of his early days.

And in September a hard-driving self-confident former Cham-ber of Commerce president, an insurance man named Roy Le-Craw, beat him in the mayor's race. It was a bitter contest, closely fought. LeCraw's attack was simple and direct. If he were elected he would stop the "hiding police" who on Hartsfield's orders lay in ambush for speeders, frequently concealing themselves behind billboards. By such tactics, LeCraw alleged, the city had collected a half million dollars in fines. He also charged that while there were thirty-six thousand registered taxpayers in the city of Atlanta, there were at least twenty thousand others who were tax-dodgers. It was no wonder, then, that Hartsfield's administration had to increase taxes by two million dollars on the honest taxpayers, LeCraw said, while taking no action against the others. Hartsfield had also raised water rates by at least 30 percent, LeCraw claimed. When *he* was elected, LeCraw promised, all these evils would be cured.

Only one of these arguments made an impression on the Atlanta voter. The "hiding police" issue touched a nerve. Hartsfield's twenty-five-mile-an-hour speed law was difficult for drivers to observe—hundreds had been arrested and fined—and it did little good for the mayor to point out that by slowing down drivers the traffic death toll had been reduced from eighty-seven fatalities in 1936 to twenty-seven in 1939. There was of course another side to the traffic story. Slow traffic sometimes *caused* accidents. When traffic began to pile up behind a dawdling motorist, frustrated drivers in the back of the line would make a run for it—and crash head on into a car coming over a hill or around a curve. Hartsfield himself got a lecture from Fulton County policemen on this subject. One July evening in 1940 two county officers noticed a Packard sedan traveling very slowly on Buford Highway, with a great many cars behind it. They managed to get to the head of the line and pulled the Packard over to the side. The driver immediately wanted to know the name of the officer who had stopped him and why he was being stopped. The officer told him he was driving so slowly that he was creating a hazard on a stretch of road where several fatal accidents had been caused by such driving. The driver then informed the officer that he never drove more than twenty-five miles an hour, whether he was driving in town or on the highway. "The operator of the car as shown by the driver's license was W. B. Hartsfield, mayor of the city of Atlanta," the officers said in their report. "In the car with Mayor Hartsfield was a young lady. We did not inquire as to her name . . . we did not make a case as no violation of the law was involved."[14] Even so, LeCraw's people heard about the incident and made copies of the officers' report, one of which reached Hartsfield and was tucked away in his files. (In passing it is worth noting that Hartsfield, for all his interest in traffic control, was a menace behind the wheel. In town he would make U-turns in the middle of the street or turn left without signaling. On the expressway if he passed his exit ramp, he would slam on the brakes and back up, while brakes screeched and horns blared behind him. One such experience so unnerved John O. Chiles that he dived forward into the front seat. Even riding with one of his two excellent chauffeurs, Charley Cook or Jimmy Winn, was an exhausting experience, for Hartsfield kept urging them to go faster, or slower, or to make a sudden turn.)

The election on September 4, 1940 was one of the closest ever to settle a mayor's race in Atlanta, and it was the consensus of political observers that the "hiding police" issue was the decisive factor. Almost equally damaging though was an issue over which Hartsfield had no control. The railroads and the newly organized pipeline companies were locked in legal combat over the right of the pipelines to cross under railroad rights-of-way. To defeat Senator Everett Millican, vice-president of Gulf Oil and proponent of the pipelines, Gurney Bayne of Southern Railway had organized a block-by-block crusade against Millican, who was a good friend of Hartsfield's. As a result, Hartsfield, to his amazement, lost to LeCraw by a margin of 83 votes. Out of nearly 23,000 ballots cast, Hartsfield had polled 11,327, LeCraw, 11,410. Hartsfield of course was outraged. He was convinced that there had been some rascality at the polls, and he set out to find who was responsible. He sought first to find out from the ward committee who had been the managers and clerks at the polls. When he was told by one committeeman that this was an "unusual request" and was asked to explain why he needed this information, his anger boiled over. "It does not occur to me that I should assign any reason for wanting to know the names of those who helped conduct the election," he wrote the committeeman. "Suppose, for instance, you were tried by a jury and were informed that you would get a fair trial, but that the judge would not let you know the names of the jurors unless you assigned a satisfactory reason to him . . . I think your letter entitles me to ask you a question, which is this—why should I be kept in the dark as to the identity of all the persons who conducted the election in your ward."[15]

Nothing came of Hartsfield's effort to contest the election, and soon it dawned on him that he had been the victim less, perhaps, of chicanery at the polls than of his own overconfidence. He thought it was obvious to everyone that he had been a great mayor. Years later he sadly reviewed his defeat. "I thought I'd done such a helluva good job I didn't need to campaign," he said. "But you've got to fight, every time. You could pave the streets with gold, reduce taxes to a nickel a year and scent the sewers with Chanel No. 5—and they wouldn't remember you unless you reminded them."[16]

Though he had been voted out of office, Hartsfield's friends saw to it that he did not lack for gainful employment. With war clouds gathering, The Coca-Cola Company had been asked by the ordnance department to build and operate a huge powder-loading plant at Talladega, Alabama. Bob Woodruff, knowing that Hartsfield had borrowed on his insurance to finance his first race for mayor—and was still paying on the note—passed the word that Hartsfield was to serve as legal consultant to the Brecon Loading Company.

Hartsfield's absence from City Hall was brief. In the spring of 1942 Mayor LeCraw put on the uniform of his country and took military leave of absence. Then in May, in a special election, Hartsfield won handily over eight other candidates. For the next two decades the office was to be his.

TOO BUSY TO HATE

HARTSFIELD first became mayor when Atlanta was just beginning to fight its way out of a depression. He took office the second time in a city at war—and soon realized that many of the things he had hoped to do would have to wait. There was the matter of the old city auditorium, for example, which seemed to be inhabited by some poltergeist determined to harass and annoy him. Soon after he first took office the auditorium roof, which had been built under the Key administration, fell in during a heavy rain. The roof was repaired, but just before he was to go out of office, the front section of the building burned. The WPA had replaced the old structure with a fireproof shell of steel and concrete. But as the war came along, making building materials for nonessential purposes impossible to obtain, Hartsfield was faced with the prospect of boarding up the windows or finishing it off with wood. His decision was to make the best of the materials that were available. It was this philosophy that sustained him, and Atlanta, throughout the war. "Steering a city through troublesome times is just like piloting a ship through stormy waters," he told a *Journal Magazine* writer. "You don't know what you are going to run into but you are going to be ready for anything. You may have to go through obstacles instead of around them. Or you may have to zigzag."[1]

One thing did not change—his determination that Atlanta should be a clean city, free of professional crooks. Big wartime payrolls, he knew, would attract the organized underworld; and his orders to the police were clear and blunt. Make it so hot for them they can't stay here. Atlanta, he told his police, had to rid itself of "all loafers and idlers and criminal parasites, whose only aim is to live upon the wages of a large number of soldiers and defense workers in our midst."[2] As a result Atlanta got the reputation among the thousands of troops that came in from the surrounding training camps of being a good "leave" town. A soldier could come into Atlanta with a few dollars in his pocket, looking for a few beers and some pleasant companionship, and be pretty well assured that he would not be robbed, rolled, ripped off, or served a Mickey in any of the local bars and pleasure palaces. Troopers seeking quieter pleasures also had reason to feel a fondness for Hartsfield's wartime Atlanta. At the Travelers' Aid desk at bus, air, and rail terminals they could find invitations to family dinners or weekend accommodations, and many lifelong friendships between Atlantans and young men from all over the nation began this way. In fact, a sizable number of the new citizens who moved into Hartsfield's Atlanta after the war were ex-military people who first saw the city, and sensed its mood and promise, when they came there on leave from Fort Benning, Fort Oglethorpe, or Camp Jackson.

To the degree that wartime restrictions would permit, Hartsfield soon fell back into the habit he had acquired during his first term as mayor. His true family was again the city, and he spent his evenings keeping a quiet eye on how it was faring. He had a two-way police radio in his car, and wherever there was a fire or accident, riot or robbery, he usually showed up, standing unobtrusively in the background, watching the police go about their work. Remembering the threats against his life during his first term of office, he carried both a pistol and a rifle in his car.

The sight of the city in all its moods and weathers fascinated him; and as an incessant taker of color movies, who felt a drive to chronicle the life of the city in pictures, he built up a notable film library. One reel of which he was particularly proud was a prewar shot of Hurt Park at night, with its colored fountains playing.

One hobby he had to give up was his habit of driving for miles through the Georgia mountains on weekends, looking for phosphates, clays, talc, and minerals; but out of his knowledge already acquired he kept up a correspondence with a number of government agencies, telling them where in Georgia useful war materials could be found. He was particularly excited about the creation of the huge Bell Bomber Plant at Marietta, which brought work to thousands of hill country Georgians who knew it as "the Boomer plant."

Like the old city auditorium, the city prison farm—known as the stockade—had been the shame of every city administration, and Hartsfield was determined to do something about it. During his first term he ordered the discharge of several employees who were considered to be drunken incompetents, and he put in a new superintendent, recommended by the University of Georgia College of Agriculture. The place was cleaned up and a more humane system of treating prisoners was put into effect. The result, according to Hartsfield, was to anger "a few cheap politicians who have vowed political vengeance"[3] for the firing of their friends or kinsmen, and the antagonism this aroused continued to harass him. However, the new superintendent, H. H. Gibson, was able to defend himself with an eloquence Hartsfield himself might envy. In a letter to George B. Lyle, chairman of the prison committee of council, in reference to a request for prisoners to work the city's streets, Gibson wrote:

About the only thing that society has offered the majority of men we handle is a bloody head and face at the hands of police, sweat of the brow from the end of a pick handle furnished by the construction department, and a liquor jug furnished by the profiteers from the blistered hands of human suffering. If the time has come when the city of Atlanta cannot keep its streets built and in repair without first considering the living conditions of the prisoner to be worked in the streets, it is about time some of us start walking. If the construction department can't get along without prison labor its doors should close in shame.[4]

Gibson's earnestness and eloquence were not lost on the grand jury investigating conditions at the stockade, and as Hartsfield came back into office they strongly supported Gibson's report, recommending that the shabby old stockade barracks be torn down and replaced. They also approved Hartsfield's judgment of Gibson—they had, they said, formed a very high opinion of Gibson's management and of the way in which he was operating the institution.

Hartsfield was quick to defend men he believed in, such as Gibson. His hand was against anyone, however, who he thought might be betraying the city in any way. As soon as he went into office in June 1942 he wrote the recruiting officers in the Atlanta area, asking them to report to Police Chief Hornsby or Fire Chief Styron the name of any Atlanta policeman or fireman who might seek to enlist in the armed services. His reasons were simple. A policeman or fireman who was facing charges for some form of misconduct could escape trial by going into the service. Then, under a city ordinance, he could come back to his old job after the war was over at the same rate of pay he had received when he left. Hartsfield wanted to close this escape hatch.

By March 1943 more than nine hundred employees of the city of Atlanta were in the armed services, and many of them wrote him homesick letters, asking for news of the old home town. He tried to answer all who wrote, giving them some paternal advice. Take a lot of pictures, he told them, of where you have been and what you have done, so that in years to come your grandchildren will listen when you tell them about the war. To some of his old newspaper friends in service he sent sixteen-millimeter movies he had taken of the city, so that they could have a nostalgic evening looking at action pictures of their old hometown. His letters to them also gave a behind-the-headlines view of what was going on in town. Moving quietly and without fanfare, Hartsfield was working through government agencies to get the auditorium finished without doing violence to War Production Board restrictions. Contrary to his usual impulse to trumpet from the housetops any good thing he did for the city, he asked the city editors of the papers not to give the project any publicity. Otherwise, he said, every school, college, store, and church in Georgia would descend upon the War Production Board, asking for the same treatment. He also was able to get the old city stockade replaced with new and more efficient buildings.

Other projects of greater scope which might be brought to fruition under pressure of the war were constantly on his mind. The war had proved the miraculous capabilities of the helicopter, and late in 1943 he wrote to Igor Sikorsky of United Aircraft, asking for technical advice on helicopter landing pads within the city. Atlanta, he told Sikorsky, was the pioneer southern city in the development of aviation, and he was determined to keep it ahead of other cities by moving to the next step in aviation—the short-range helicopter. (How well Hartsfield's pioneering in this new mode of flight succeeded can be seen and heard today over downtown Atlanta.) While pushing for the helicopter he was by no means neglecting his first love —the airport—and he acquired some eight hundred acres of adjacent land so that the runways could be extended. His reasoning: Lockheed bombers might need an alternate airport on a cloudy day—and the longer runways, once built, could handily serve the larger planes of the future.

One favorite project did not materialize. In 1942 he wrote Major John T. Carlton, once the *Journal's* city hall reporter and perhaps the mayor's closest confidant among the journalists, that he once more was trying to sell the north side on annexation, and that this time he was getting more help from prominent outsiders—meaning some of the business interests living in the Buckhead area. "I am putting it on the basis of preserving the town for decent people," he said, "and this argument is hard to offset."[5]

To get his point across, Hartsfield had written a letter to several hundred Atlantans. The letter, addressed only to "Gentlemen," pointed out that if Buckhead were actually brought into the city, its residents would get better services at less cost. The annexation movement, Hartsfield said, was not for revenue purposes at all. It was a movement for better government. The city wanted voters, not money. "The most important thing to remember," he wrote, "cannot be publicized in the press or made the subject of public speeches. Our Negro population is growing by leaps and bounds. They stay right in the city limits and grow by taking more white territory inside Atlanta. Outmigration is good, white, homeowning citizens. With the federal government insisting on political recognition of Negroes in local affairs, the time is not far distant when they will become a potent political force in Atlanta if our white citizens are just going to move out and give it to them. This is not intended to stir race prejudice because all of us want to deal fairly with them; but do you want to hand them political control of Atlanta?" (The leaders of the black power structure were well aware, of course, of Hartsfield's attitude toward their increasing political potency. But they were aware, too, that for all his reservations, there were in him deep wells of political wisdom, which in time would cause him to modify his views.)

To Hartsfield's distress, the "county politicians and the Buckhead merchants" were not persuaded by his arguments. Annexation did not pass. On June 18, 1943, he reported to a former city hall clerk, Major Charles M. Ford, Jr., that "the Fulton rep-

resentative got cold feet on us with the Buckhead annexation
and declined to pass the bill."

Nobody, it might be added, had a deeper sympathy for the
Negro in his helpless and dependent role than did Hartsfield.
In one case, because he knew the man's mother, he spent time,
money, and prodigious effort in getting the death sentence of
a black murderer commuted. He often expressed the opinion
that the black man charged with a capital crime had little
chance of survival. Usually penniless, he was assigned the
youngest, most ignorant, and least well trained lawyers, and a
white jury had little interest in getting at the truth in cases in
which only blacks were involved. In the case of this man, Lint
Reed, Hartsfield, after helping bring about the commutation of
Reed's sentence, wrote the Pardons and Parole Board: "If he
had been a white man, and had a good lawyer, he would have
been exonerated with thanks—and I have always criticized myself for not taking a greater interest in him, and allowing him to
go to trial without aiding him in the preparation of his case."[6]
He then spent several more months trying to get Reed moved
from Tattnall prison to Fulton County, where he could be near
his mother.

Not all of Hartsfield's concerns were matters of life and death
or geographical boundaries. Wartime gas and rubber rationing
cut down the flow of angry visitors to his office, but the mails
were heavier than ever. One outraged wife wrote Hartsfield demanding that he close the Elks' Club because her husband
could go there to drink on Sunday. Another citizen, a grande
dame living in one of the elegant apartments at Peachtree and
Ponce de Leon, demanded that Hartsfield silence Ernie Marrs,
a *Constitution* newsboy with an ear-shattering voice, who
dressed in a dinner jacket to shout the headlines on nights when
the Metropolitan Opera was playing at the Fox Theater across
the street. Parents harassed the mayor, asking him to use his

influence to get their drafted sons into officer school, or to get them into medical school, or the veterinary corps, so that they could practice the healing rather than the lethal arts. Because of the tire shortage the city had to stop hauling leaves, limbs, and hedge cuttings, causing a great outcry from property owners, leading Hartsfield to conclude that some folks would complain about the leaf pickup even if Hitler were at the city limits.

One wartime campaign in particular fired his imagination and enlisted his whole support. The cruiser *Atlanta*, christened by Margaret Mitchell on September 6, 1941, went down after a gallant fight off Guadalcanal in December 1942; 172 men were killed and 79 wounded. Immediately in the city a war bond drive was begun to raise $35 million to build a new *Atlanta*. The drive was so successful that $165 million in bonds were sold. At Hartsfield's suggestion to the Secretary of the Navy, Miss Mitchell again was asked to be the sponsor. At her request, Mayor Hartsfield, for his diligent labors on behalf of the bond sales, was asked to be a member of the official party at the launching; and at the request of both of them, Lieutenant Commander DeSales Harrison, a former Atlantan, was asked to function as Miss Mitchell's naval aide. When she asked Harrison what was the function of a naval aide, he explained that it was to see that the seams of the sponsor's stockings were straight.

The launching of this, the fourth ship to bear the name *Atlanta*, took place at Camden, New Jersey, on December 3, 1944. For Hartsfield it was a peak moment as he stood with Peggy, Lieutenant Commander Harrison, and Captain B. H. Colyear, the new ship's commander, on the launching platform. His presence not only got his picture in the papers, it also entitled him to a Plank Owner's Certificate, decorated with mermaids and sea horses, which granted him "clear and unencumbered title to one plank in the weather deck" and to all the privileges due a member of the original crew that commissioned the ship.

This fourth *Atlanta* served through the closing days of the war, joining in the bombardment of Japan. Hartsfield was a sentimental man about anything that had to do with the history of his city. The silver punch bowl that the city had given the third *Atlanta* had been lost in the Guadalcanal battle, but the ancient bowl that had been part of the silver service of the 1886 *Atlanta* was still floating around somewhere in the Navy. It was located and at Hartsfield's request was placed aboard the fourth *Atlanta*. In 1959 it finally came home, a gift of the Navy, and is now on display at the Atlanta Historical Society. (The first *Atlanta* was a Confederate ironclad captured by federal forces in 1863.)

Hartsfield stopped off in Washington on his way home from the launching to talk to people in the federal government, and he warned them, amiably, that he would be calling on them for help in putting into effect Atlanta's plans for expansion after the war. Actually Hartsfield, when visiting other cities to find out what they had in mind for the future, had discovered that Atlanta, during the war, had already accomplished much that similar cities still looked upon as post-war projects. Grady Hospital's facilities had been expanded with the addition of a nurse's home and a clinic for the treatment of syphilis by fever therapy, which Hartsfield hoped would rid Atlanta of the unhappy reputation of being the venereal disease capital of the world. Worried about juvenile delinquency, he had pushed for parks and playground areas for both white and black citizens. Fifteen miles of streets had been resurfaced, and at the new city farm prison, a fine new detention hospital had been built. (Hartsfield was thinking of his old friend Lint Reed, the Negro murderer, suffering from paresis, with no prison hospital in the county to care for him.)

Things had been happening in Atlanta late in the war, however, that caused Hartsfield grave concern. It seemed to him that there was a growing tendency in the country to "put down" the South—a mood that might well endanger his chances of getting strong federal help, after the war, for the ten million dollars in civic projects he already had in the blueprint stage. Early in 1944 he wrote to Martin Dies, chairman of the congressional committee charged with the investigation of subversive organizations, asking him to look into the affairs of the National Association for the Advancement of Colored People. He had no evidence, he said, but he was of the opinion that a lot of the "professional white agitators . . . who were . . . stirring up racial questions in the South, especially among educators, church people, and women's groups," were being surreptitiously supported by the NAACP.[7] A month later, on April 10, 1944, he went on WSB radio to deliver a fiery denunciation of a federal judge in Chicago who had made the public assertion that the hills of Georgia constituted the most backward section in America. To Hartsfield this was just one more instance of what he called "an organized campaign of vilification and derision of Southern people, their customs and historic traditions." He came on the air with the thunder of Confederate cannon in his voice. The judge's gratuitous comment, he said, had come about while sentencing a couple under the White Slave Act for having brought a north Georgia girl to Chicago for immoral purposes. "The place of this sordid crime was in the judge's home community. It furnished the evil conditions and the ready market for the shame of this Georgia girl." But by implication Chicago was held up as a progressive place, while the hills of Georgia, whose only offense was to produce the child, were held up to the nation as the most backward section in the nation.

Hartsfield then turned his considerable capacity for invective on Chicago, whose contribution to social uplift, he said, was represented by Al Capone and other gangsters. Chicago, he continued, had other flaws. "In the dangerous days when our nation was trying to rearm itself and prepare for the coming

Willie Hartsfield, age 7.
His father shined his shoes; his mother curled his hair.

Still a dandy at age 23. Hartsfield and his wife Pearl,
on a bridge in Grant Park in their early, happy years.

At age 26, he reads law in the prestigious Atlanta firm
of Rosser, Slaton, Phillips and Hopkins. His general education
came from his alma mater, the public library.

An aerial view of the fledgling airport, circa 1928,
which Hartsfield fathered.

aggression of the dictators, men and women were parading the streets of the judge's home community, criticizing our government and stirring up disunity. At the same time in Georgia boys were voluntarily enlisting in the armed forces to a greater degree than any other part of the nation, and it was in the hill country of the South that our government found its quickest and most vigorous response to its foreign policy."

He then turned to the subject that now obsessed him—the "intolerant and provocative abuse" from "so-called liberals, alleged sociologists, advanced educators, agitators, left wing radicals and South haters," who were flooding the nation and the South with ceaseless propaganda. They were well-heeled, he said, from "funds set up by men with more money than common sense"; they had the support of magazines of national circulation and the favor of the extension departments of great northern universities, some of whose faculties, he said, had become enamoured with certain foreign ideas of government.

He did not pretend that all Georgians were perfect, nor were they allergic to progress. On the contrary, he said, "Georgians have made great progress in social affairs, and will continue to do so, but we will do it in a calm orderly way and within the framework of Southern wisdom and experience." Though the North's "professional bleeding hearts, agitators, and fevered-brow social uplifters see in us a lot of benighted hill-billies whom they are going to save and make over to their own, and usually foreign, specifications," Hartsfield said, this was not the attitude of all the North. "Indeed," he said, "a great majority of level-headed, sensible Northern people feel pretty much as we Southerners do about our problems. Thousands of them have come to live with us and be a part of us, and they almost always adopt the Southern viewpoint, when first-hand experience and not radical propaganda becomes their guide."

Finally, Hartsfield came to the main point of his broadcast, a plea for "real, sensible and constructive tolerance . . . which manifests itself in everyday friendly relationships with those who live about and around us." At the last of course there must come the classic peroration required of any Southern orator, and in Hartsfield's closing were echoes of every Memorial Day speech he had ever heard. First, the tribute to the men and women who followed Lee and Jackson, who survived the hardships of Reconstruction, who accepted the bitter fruits of defeat at arms without complaint. Then the tribute to Southern womanhood: "My own mother," he thundered, "knew what it was to go into the woods to forage for wild berries and fruits after invading armies had stripped them of everything they had." "But these Southern people," he continued, "had something that no armies could conquer . . . character, common sense, and a willingness to work . . . [and] the story of their bitter and unaided struggle to raise themselves once more to full manhood and womanhood in the Union forms one of the greatest sagas of modern civilization."

When this mood was upon him, Hartsfield was still the unreconstructed Rebel, one in spirit with his Confederate ancestors and as bitter in his hatred of "fevered-brow" intellectuals preaching the end of segregation as his forebears had been in their denunciation of abolitionists preaching the end of slavery. Yet, in this time, Hartsfield was going through what many other southerners were enduring, a wrenching and twisting of spiritual moorings. There was in him, too, an instinct for fair play, a growing realization that the quiet counsel he was receiving from his "Kitchen Cabinet" of black advisors was correct. The day of the arrant white supremacist was over; the black man could no longer be held down because of his color, deprived of the opportunity to reach his full potential, in education, in economics, and above all, in politics. It was to the "go-slow, go-easy, but go" philosophy of Ellis Arnall and Carl Sanders, rather than to the militant resistance policies of Marvin Griffin and Lester Maddox, that Hartsfield turned as he laid his plans for Atlanta's future. This dichotomy naturally left him vulnerable to the extremes of both left and right. To the Klan and the Columbians and the White Citizens' Councils he was, in the harsh phrase of the times, a nigger-lover. To the more hot-eyed integrationists he was, at best, a Jim Crow liberal.

Either way, of one thing he was resolved—that Atlanta would move forward without violence. With his genius for capsuling a moment of history in a phrase, he came up with a slogan that captured the imagination of most Atlantans and of all the nation outside the South. Atlanta, he said, was "a city too busy to hate."

And that was indeed the mood of Atlanta during the surging years of growth that followed World War II. There were sit-ins and demonstrations, and a temple was bombed. But in the long run, the busy, booming city handled with a minimum of disruption the violent civil-rights issues that set angry whites and marching blacks in bloody confrontation in the streets of many of her sister cities of the South.

It is difficult to know just when Hartsfield's slow metamorphosis in racial attitudes began, so gradual was his conversion. In the beginning of his political career he was the typical segregationist of his time. He became, in his own proud boast, the "mayor of all the people," taking the first small hesitant steps toward racial understanding. His first efforts were tentative. Instead of removing "white" and "colored" signs from restrooms at the airport, he first had them reduced in size until they could hardly be seen. Finally, with no notice given, they disappeared. He required municipal clerks, when sending letters to black citizens, to address them as Mr., Mrs., or Miss, and there was grumbling at City Hall when this order came down. (This was a typical Southern white hangup. A black man could comfortably be addressed as "Doctor" or "Professor," but "Mister" was taboo.)

Possibly the change began with his memory of his mother

telling him that the duty of a man in public office was to help those who were trying to help themselves. Possibly it was the sight of black soldiers from the North, coming to Atlanta during the war, surprised and bewildered when told that they could not sit down to eat in a "white" restaurant or ride the front seats of a city bus. More likely, though, the great light dawned when in 1946 a Texas court outlawed the white primary. The significance of this was clear enough to a man with Hartsfield's instinct for politics. It meant that the voting patterns would never again be the same in the South. The black leaders knew as well as did Hartsfield that the ballot would open doors long closed to them. Under the voting restrictions that had existed, fewer than three hundred blacks had bothered to register. Now, at the Butler Street YMCA—the nerve center of decision-making among blacks—Grace Hamilton, A. T. Walden, Warren Cochran, and others from that area invited Hartsfield to talk to them about black problems. It was simple, he pointed out, "your vote will buy you a ticket to any place you want to sit."[8] And concerning their specific problems, if they should come to him with ten thousand black votes, he would be glad to listen to what they had to say. Led by Mrs. Hamilton, guided by Dr. Clarence A. Bacote of Atlanta University, who knew the census tracts, they put eighteen thousand names on the voters' list in fifty-one days. By 1949 there were twenty-five thousand blacks registered, and every politician in Atlanta wooed them. Hartsfield though was the man who won them. Through his sense of the dramatic, his humor, his charismatic appeal, he held the black vote through all the years he was in office.

He moved slowly and with the utmost care to get them the recognition that they wanted. The greatest tension between the races derived from the relationship of the black man to the white police. Black crime against a black might be ignored. Black crime against a white person would be punished, first on the street with the utmost brutality, and then in the courts. The leaders of the Negro community, since Mayor Key's time, had urged the creation of a black force to police the black communities. Key favored this but knew that a Klan-dominated police force would never permit it. Hartsfield, whose police force had been purged of active Klansmen, knew that at last the time was ripe. So did his highly capable police chief, Herbert Jenkins. So did Councilman Ralph Huie and other powerful members of council. Moving slowly, selecting the candidates with utmost care, Hartsfield and Jenkins finally made their move. In the spring of 1948 eight black men in uniform, the first Negro policemen in the city of Atlanta, began walking their beats. It seemed as if the whole Negro community turned out to see them. Silent at first, then shouting for joy and pride, they marched along with the new black recruits. Hartsfield and Chief Jenkins, following what had suddenly turned into a joyous parade, looked at each other and smiled. They had gambled and won.

Here, too, at first there were limitations. The blacks reported to the Butler Street YMCA instead of the police station on Decatur Street. They changed into their uniforms there, and they were not allowed to put a white person under arrest. Hartsfield later was to use his black officers most effectively as stage props in his campaigns. He would appear to speak before a black rally, and all of a sudden the black policemen in full uniform would appear, to the loud applause of the black audience. One of his favorite ploys, particularly when campaigning against his perennial opponent, Charlie Brown, was to wait outside a Negro mass meeting until Brown was in the middle of his speech. He would then enter with his entourage, to loud applause, shaking hands right and left and leaving the hapless speaker frothing in rage.

From the blacks' standpoint, the appointment of black policemen was the first real breakthrough in race relations in

Atlanta, and it was a matter of pride to Hartsfield that this truly progressive step—for a southern city—was brought off so smoothly. The restriction on a black officer arresting a white person soon was lifted, and the idea of the black policeman enforcing the law became so acceptable to Atlantans that eventually the city was to have a black police commissioner and the greatest percentage of blacks on its police force of any major city in the country, North or South.

Two years before the first black officer appeared on the streets, Hartsfield's handling of an explosive situation had given the black community some encouragement. In 1946 the presence in Atlanta of a racist hate organization called the Columbians had brought momentary shame and embarrassment to the city, but Hartsfield's police chief, then a stern old man named Marion Hornsby, quietly put them down. The Columbians would patrol neighborhoods, presumably "keeping the peace" but actually seeking to intimidate blacks who had the audacity to move into a white area. To Hornsby the issue was simple. Either his police or the Columbians would keep the peace in Atlanta. Faced with jail the Columbians faded from the civic scene. Not long afterward Hornsby died and was replaced by Herbert Jenkins, who soon became almost as much a symbol of Atlanta as the mayor himself.

ENEMIES WITHOUT, WITHIN

SUCH HOMEGROWN ZEALOTS as the Klan or the Columbians, or even the county chauvinists who fought the expansion of the city, did not disturb Hartsfield as much as did those whom he believed to be members of an international plot to destroy the democracies. He used every means at his disposal to ferret them out. He wrote Georgia's congressmen asking for the names of any Atlantans bringing pressure on them to support the FEPC; he wrote his good friend Gerald P. O'Hara, bishop of Savannah-Atlanta, on special duty at the Vatican, about his concern. The bishop replied that he, like Hartsfield, had long suspected that communists had infiltrated certain Protestant churches, so subtly that their influence was barely perceptible, and that this bode no good for the future of the non-Catholic churches in the United States. As for the Catholics, he indicated that they were well aware of this communist movement wherever it might be taking place. He had always known, the bishop said, that the Vatican was well informed, but in the past six weeks he had had access to confidential files and had been "utterly amazed at the absolute accuracy, thoroughness, and abundance of information that the Holy See possesses for every country in the world."[1] All of this information, he told Hartsfield, was available to the president of the United States through Myron Taylor, the president's personal representative to Pope Pius XII,

and should be of great help to the chief executive and his associates in directing their global diplomacy. The bishop gathered
from Hartsfield's letter that the mayor shared his view that
Taylor should not be recalled, thus breaking the contact that
was of such value to the United States in formulating its policies toward other countries.

Hartsfield, a devout Baptist, was held in high esteem by the
Catholics, who often invited him to speak to them on important
occasions such as a fund-raising drive for a Catholic hospital.
He always accepted readily, but, for the benefit of his Protestant electorate, he always mentioned his Baptist affiliations.

In 1946, at the dinner launching the fund drive for Saint
Joseph's Infirmary, the oldest hospital in Atlanta, Hartsfield
described it as a "monument to the Catholic citizenship of Atlanta, who have long been in the forefront of those . . . civic
activities which have contributed so much to Atlanta's growth."
As a Baptist mayor, he said, he was glad to pay tribute to those
fine pioneers who established Saint Joseph's. But, he went on,
they might find him in the position of the old Negro Mammy
from south Georgia, who moved North, was knocked down by
an automobile in a snow storm, and was carried to a Catholic
hospital. There a nursing sister slipped a little crucifix in her
hand as she was wheeled into the operating room. Before the
ether put her out, she was heard to murmur a prayer. "Oh
Lord, take care of this old Mammy and don't let me die. But
don't be fooled by what I is holding in my hand, 'cause I is still
a Baptist."[2]

Whatever his forum, Hartsfield never failed to beat the drum
for Atlanta. In his talk to the Catholics he pointed out that the
building of a new hospital was only one of many improvements
the city needed. It was, he said, many years behind in water
main and meter installation, office buildings, business and industrial space. Metropolitan Atlanta, he said, was literally burst-
ing at the seams; it must expand or die. New housing was

greatly needed, but Hartsfield was particular about what *kind* of housing was to be put up. He was for slum clearance, but the unrelenting enemy of "those selfish greedy builders who want to take advantage of those desperate for space by foisting off cheap, flimsy houses on war veterans and others for enormous, quick profits." Such builders, he said, were pressing the building inspector and city council to relax the building code so they could ruin residential areas with their small cheap slums of the future. Other irresponsible contractors, Hartsfield said, "follow the city inspectors like vultures, preying on landlords and little people in poor sections, whose construction, electrical work or plumbing had been condemned, and who hope to get rich by doing poor work at fabulous prices." Atlanta, Hartsfield admitted, must have low-cost housing for its poorer people, but it must be well planned, well built, and so financed, preferably by private capital, if not by the federal government, that it may be rented at prices the poor could afford to pay.

Hartsfield's success in guiding his city through the war and the first years thereafter made his name well known both in Washington and nationally, and he was constantly being called on to use his influence in one cause or another. The Association of Los Alamos Scientists sent him a sample of desert sand, fused into glass by the first atomic bomb, along with a picture of the devastation caused at Nagasaki. Willard Stout, for the committee, asked Hartsfield to put the glass on display, "to remind the people of Atlanta that in another war their city would probably be destroyed in the first hours of the conflict by atomic explosions dropped from the air by guided rockets, or previously hidden in some cellars by enemy agents." He also asked that Hartsfield testify in Washington in favor of international control of atomic weapons, since no adequate defense against these devices existed or was likely to be developed in the near future.

This set Hartsfield off on a discourse in which he seemed to disagree with the idea of international control. He wrote Stout:

You and your fellow scientists know more about the bomb than I do, or probably ever will, but it seems to me, in my present state of ignorance, that we should adopt a policy of dignified leadership, sureness and forthrightness, born out of the realization that a Divine Providence has seen fit to trust US with this awesome power.

I don't want to see us put into the position of trembling in cowardly fright and running to other less idealistic, but more crafty and cunning world leaders, begging them for cooperation, on the score that we will never use atomic bombs, but they might when they got the secret.

Both the strength and weakness of this great nation lies in its complete openness and accessibility in all human and physical affairs. The world can see us, know us and examine us in the minutest detail. But can we do the same in Russia? Until we can see and know each other in minute detail, how can we be sure of mutual cooperation.

To be perfectly frank, this individual can never have any feeling of trust for a land which is sealed off from the outside world and whose propagandists are constantly stirring trouble in our midst. That is not even the faintest beginning of world cooperation. I would rather take my chance on the power of my own country in the atomic field, than trust such a country. When they, like us, grant individual freedom and elevate the individual and not the State, then we will have a basis for world cooperation.

Like many others I am sorry atomic energy was made possible, but since it was I am glad it was us and hope for the time being we will make and store it bigger and better than the balance of the world, thereby enabling us to adopt the attitude of forthright leadership in world affairs.

Noting that the piece of glass was slightly radioactive, he turned it over to the state museum, along with Mr. Stout's ominous message, rather than putting it on display at City Hall.

Hartsfield's response often dismayed those who called upon him for help. To the Palestine resistance fighters, who were bringing brutal pressure upon a weakened British force trying to bring about a peaceful solution to the Palestine problem under relentless pressure from Jews determined to return to their ancient homeland, Hartsfield's reply was harsh: "Do I understand you are asking me for money to help promote a group of terrorists who are dynamiting buildings, challenging the authority of organized government and generally playing Stalin's game in the Middle East . . . As a friend of the Jewish people I think they are doing the cause of world wide Jewry great harm."[3] He sent a copy of his letter to a Jewish friend in Atlanta, Julian Boehm, who had shared with him the spotlight at the *Gone with the Wind* celebration. Boehm sent back a highly approving note, saying, "Bill, you are absolutely correct in all that you wrote those people, that the Zionist Group did not approve such resistance groups, but considered them outlaw organizations."

There were other matters of global scope that enlisted Hartsfield's heartiest support. When a distinguished committee of both Republicans and Democrats requested him to sign a petition urging Congress promptly to pass legislation supporting the Marshall Plan to aid Europe's recovery, he signed immediately, and wrote that anything done now, no matter how costly, would be cheap if it kept the world from chaos.

Occasionally a seemingly trivial request would set him off upon a long discussion of the joys and trials of being mayor. An editor of *Kiplinger Magazine* wrote to ask him about his attitude toward passing out keys to the city. He answered that sometimes a movie press agent, for publicity purposes, would have a big wooden key made, and he of course would happily do the honors. But for distinguished guests, all the city's doors were already unlocked, and there was no need for any keys. He then went into a general discussion of a mayor's ceremonial duties.

Of course the Mayor of most cities has a long and varied list of visitors to greet. There is the usual contingent of presidents of companies with branches located in the city, motion picture stars, queens of this and that, and other assorted celebrities. In my case I have welcomed the President of the United States, three Latin American Presidents, a large number of movie stars, the Twenty-Millionth Ford, Elsie the Cow, and Bess, the M.G.M. horse, which latter was marched into my office. This occasioned the remark from me that it was the first time I had ever had a whole horse in my office. Of course there is also the usual round of visits laying cornerstones, snipping ribbons, opening new shows and exhibits, pitching the first balls, ground breakings and all of the other publicity stunts which, by common custom, the Mayor is supposed to do.

As you know, many cities have the Manager form of government, but also have a Mayor whose duties are largely ceremonial. This is in recognition of the fact that the American public simply will not be denied the services of the head man.

Because he was a working mayor, rather than a ceremonial mayor who turned over to a city manager the management of its government, Hartsfield found it "a real problem to carry on all this publicity stuff with the increasing demands of the office."[4]

One publicity picture, which caused him to beam as joyously as he had when welcoming Vivian Leigh and Clark Gable, was taken when his daughter Mildred, Mrs. J. M. Cheshire, brought his grandson, Monty, age three and a half months, to visit his office. Monty, looking solemn, clutched the mayor's tie in one hand and the mayor's gavel in his other while his grandpa grinned happily. Well knowing the publicity value of this variant of the baby-kissing technique, Hartsfield used Monty as a political prop for years thereafter.

Hartsfield throughout his career was masterful in his handling of the press, whether local, national, or foreign. He had an aptitude for public relations as uncanny as his instinct for knowing how to please a voter. This did not mean that he always tried to please the press, nor did they try to please him when they thought he was wrong, as they often did. No one ever questioned his honesty, or his commitment to doing what he thought was best for the city of Atlanta. They did often deplore the arrogance of his methods, his overweening assumption that whatever he did or said or thought had the blessing of the Almighty. He was particularly acerbic in his attitude toward newspaper management. The fact that the two papers, in nearly every campaign, gave him strong editorial support did not mollify him. Nobody read editorials, he would argue, and those who did paid little attention to them. Voters made up their minds by what they read about a candidate in the news columns—and the papers persisted in giving news coverage to his opponents, who were obviously rascals.

Though Hartsfield had one of the canniest of all public relations advisors in Helen Bullard of Charles Rawson and Associates, he was in essence his own public-relations man. When he was in what reporters described as his 3-Z mood—expansive, philosophic, amiable, reflective, generous—he would come into the pressroom in his shirt-sleeves, an unlighted cigar in his hand, sit down, put his feet on the desk, and talk with the utmost amiability. When the dark moods were upon him, though, he looked on every journalist as his enemy. Once, in a fit of anger, he ordered Howard Monroe, city hall building superintendent, to move the pressroom from the second floor near his office to an editorial Siberia on the fourteenth floor. He was tired, he said, of some damned reporter sticking his head around the door every time he had a visitor.

He always read the early editions of both papers, and if something appeared therein that displeased him, he did not send some underling over with a note of mild protest. He would immediately pounce upon the paper's city hall reporter, demanding that the story or editorial be corrected before another edition went to press. If the reporter was not around City Hall or at the paper, he would track him down at home, or in whatever bar he might have taken refuge. If he were really stirred up, he would not bother with the small fry. He would clap his hat on and head directly for the newspaper office. There he would go roaring into the presence of the highest editorial official he could find, shouting and banging on tables and demanding that a correction or retraction be printed in the next edition. Once he and George Biggers, boss of both papers and himself an irascible man, were on the verge of grappling when startled underlings pulled them apart. Editor Ralph McGill, in a way, was less fortunate than Biggers. He went home when the early edition of the *Constitution* went to press, and Hartsfield would call him there, interrupting his dinner with a shouted diatribe demanding the offending story be dropped or fixed. Then Hartsfield would sit up with Tommy Read at the Fox Theater, or some other political crony around town, until the last edition came out. If the story still did not suit him, he would call McGill again, rousing him from his bed at 2 A.M.

Every Atlanta newspaperman who knew Hartsfield in his heyday has some still vibrant memory of either his sharp wit or his temper tantrums, the latter of which sometimes caused him great embarrassment. One night, for example, he strolled jauntily into the *Constitution* city room after making a speech to an organization of working folk on the south side of town, sat down across from the reporter who had covered the meeting, took off his flat-brimmed hard straw hat and put it on the desk, and demanded amiably to know what the reporter had thought of his speech. The reporter pondered a moment and then said that he thought Mr. Hartsfield had sounded like a damned demagogue. It was unworthy of a mayor of Atlanta, he said, to try to turn the people of different sections and different economic classes against each other. He read from his notes Hartsfield's statement that "all those rich Northsiders want to do is ride through town in their Cadillacs going sixty miles an hour, running over your children and mine."[5] Hartsfield sprang to his feet, his eyes flashing with rage. He began to shout and pound on the desk, and glaring at the reporter, he crashed his fist down on his own straw hat and smashed it into a dozen pieces. There was a great roar of laughter from all the desks around, and Hartsfield, after a long and anguished moment, joined in.

Occasionally, though, Hartsfield's mood was strangely tolerant, even of the New Deal, which he believed was breaking down the national character by destroying honesty, thrift, industry, and respect for law. He would stress the need for calmness on the part of everybody—politicians, the people, the press. What the world needed more than anything else, he would argue, was for people to quit fuming and fussing and worrying over trifles, getting excited over little details that didn't amount to a row of turnips, upsetting the digestion and the disposition fighting over something when it didn't matter a tinker's dam who won the fight. When a man in public life loses his temper, he pointed out, he loses what Kipling called "the common touch" and thereby loses his contact with the people.

Once, when haranguing the city hall reporters along this line, Hartsfield's secretary, Joe Gregg, came in and laid a paper on his desk. It was a mild criticism, by a city councilman, of some action taken by the police department—a matter of relatively small consequence. But Hartsfield read into it a criticism of his newly appointed police chief, M. A. Hornsby. He sprang to his feet and threw down his cigar. He pounded the desk, he shouted, and his face turned red. His comments on the erring councilman were blasphemous. Suddenly, he stopped and looked around sheepishly—and grinned, "As Kipling was saying . . ."[6]

The reporters liked Hartsfield for his volatile streak and were sorry when his temper sometimes got him into trouble. During his race against Roy LeCraw in 1945, for example, he hurt himself with the public when he saw a man writing "Vote for Le-Craw" slogans on the sidewalk. Hartsfield, enraged, jumped out of his car, denounced the man—who turned out to be a war veteran—and had him arrested for defacing public property.

Many matters, both public and personal, concerned Hartsfield in this springboard year of 1945. Out of his vast interest in Georgia minerals he persuaded the state geologist, Garland Peyton, to help the Georgia Marble Company make a mineral survey of the talc area, for the purpose of locating future marble sites. He wrote to Congressman John Wood in Washington, offering him one dollar a ton for a kind of flint rock which lay in boulders around the congressman's farm in Pickens County and which Hartsfield thought would be useful in the manufacture of firebrick. Unhappily, tests on the samples Hartsfield sent off turned out to be unsatisfactory. The promise that oil might be found in south Georgia led him to invest in oil leases in Lowndes and Telfair counties—none of which proved out. He also began pushing again for another of his favorite projects that never came off—the development of the Chattahoochee River for navigation.

One achievement particularly pleased him, though. The Georgia legislature agreed to a bill sponsored by the Fulton and DeKalb delegations—but originally set in motion by Hartsfield, and his bitterest political enemy Charlie Brown—which would provide for the completion of the Stone Mountain Memorial. To Hartsfield, instinctively a showman, completion of the carving would not only pay a debt to the honored Confederate dead, it would provide a focal point for a tourist attraction to be developed in a two-mile radius around the mountain which would bring thousands of visitors to Atlanta every year. It would, he said, be not only a fitting monument to our honored past but visible evidence that we in the South face the future with a brilliant and flaming spirit.

While Hartsfield was thinking on the grand scale about his plans for the city, he was making some adjustments in his own life-style. In 1943 he had moved his family from 300 Milledge Avenue, in the Grant Park section, to 637 Pelham Road N.E., in Morningside, a somewhat more affluent neighborhood. It was a move that delighted his daughter Mildred, whose friends all lived on the north side. Hartsfield in his new location was no

Hartsfield celebrates with some of his political supporters, 1937.

Courtesy of the Atlanta Historical Society

Courtesy of the Woodruff Library, Emory University

Hartsfield takes the oath of office for his first term as mayor from Judge Paul Etheridge, 1937.

The new mayor and his family.
Left to right, son William B. Jr., daughter Mildred, Pearl, and Mayor Hartsfield.

Courtesy of the Atlanta Historical Society

Peachtree Street in 1938, during Hartsfield's first term in office.

more of a homebody than he had been before. He still spent most of his evenings prowling the town by car or visiting with his political cronies. His wife, Pearl, had campaigned with him in his earliest forays into politics, but now increasing ill health and a declining interest in politics made her almost a recluse. She stayed home, answered the telephone with the calm impersonality of a secretary, and nursed whatever ailing Hartsfield, Dagnall, or Williams kin might drop in. Their son, William, was of particular concern to both of them, for he suffered from chronic asthma and a severe case of Bright's disease.

Though his immediate family often felt neglected by him, Hartsfield felt a responsibility to his Hartsfield and Dagnall kin throughout Georgia and Alabama. It fell upon him to keep up the Dagnall plot in the cemetery in Kingston, where his mother's ancestors were buried; and he took on the burden of helping get on the old-age pension rolls a proud and independent cousin who stubbornly refused to admit that she was penniless. She had her "boarders" who paid her rent, she said, not knowing that Hartsfield and her brothers were paying the boarders to stay with her.

Sometimes problems came from unidentifiable sources. For several years prominent people around town, with whom Hartsfield was in some way associated, received anonymous postcards written in red ink, accusing Hartsfield of all manner of illegal acts. One card to Ralph McGill told him that Hartsfield had made strong derogatory remarks about him, causing McGill to write Hartsfield an angry letter. A card to Dr. Louie D. Newton, Baptist minister, charged Hartsfield with being controlled by the liquor interests. In a letter to M. H. Ackerman, chief postal inspector, Hartsfield said: "I realize that in some respects it seems small and ridiculous for one in my position to notice such attacks, which generally speaking are the lot of any official in the public eye . . . However, when they continue over a period of five or six years, seeming to come from one common source and resulting in trouble and misunderstandings, I certainly think the time has come to put a stop to it." Hartsfield was on the horns of a dilemma. He did not want publicity given to the anonymous attacks, for false though they were, they would stick in the public mind. Thus he concluded his letter to Ackerman with the plea that "surely your department can find a way to locate the author and have it stopped."[7]

With such diverse problems preying on him it is not strange, then, that behind the confident and ebullient facade he showed the public, Hartsfield was often a deeply harassed and troubled man. Still the matters that concerned him most were not those personally affecting him, or those close to him by blood, but those that affected the city of Atlanta. Late in 1945 he wrote to the *Journal's* Washington correspondent, Ken Turner, telling him that he had heard through the grapevine that the Alabama delegation in Congress, along with the governor of Alabama, were planning a campaign to have several federal agencies moved from Atlanta, notably the regional office of the Social Security Board. This of course was unthinkable, and the Georgia delegation must be warned to watch out for such piracy. In addition he told Turner, "all sorts of rumors are in the air about our election laws" (the white primary), the FBI had been interrogating members of the city executive committee, and there were rumors that certain election managers were to be indicted. "I am just hoping," he concluded, "that they don't push their digging too far, and pressure an open clash in the South."[8]

As did many others, he attributed these political problems to the communists, who he said were obviously "hoping for a world communist state to evolve out of the chaos of Europe." In a letter to Representative Eugene Cox, congratulating him on the creation of "another Dies Committee," he wrote:

We must still watch their agents and fellow-travelers over here. Of course the radicals and sneer-and-jeer artists will leave, but rest assured that millions of honest Americans will approve. They have few sources of national expression now, but they are still around and especially in our Southland. If this committee is set up again but not controlled by any radical influence, I would like to see it go into the sources of propaganda being spread through the South, and also find out who is paying some of these Southern "missionaries" and "agitators" who make a sensible solution of our race problems so hard.[9]

There is some evidence that Hartsfield's concern about communist influence led him to seek means of quiet surveillance. A memo to Ernest Brewer, his secretary, asked him to keep a file on supplies of wiretapping equipment used by military intelligence and to "find out where we can get phonograph recording equipment . . . [the] kind that records from a concealed mike in a desk, and from cells upstairs in police stations, etc."

His concern about the jeerers and sneerers, however, was far less than his pride in the way his city, and the state of Georgia, had supported the war effort. In seven war bond campaigns Georgia had bought more than one-and-a-half-billion-dollars' worth of bonds—and Atlantans alone had subscribed to one half of that. In the eighth campaign, the Victory Loan Drive, Hartsfield made a fine plea. No city, he said, is any stronger than its contributors to the general welfare of the nation and to the welfare of all the people of the country. The interest of a city in a bond campaign is as vital as its interest in sewage disposal, fire fighting, or city finances.

Hartsfield told his listeners that he had made a bet with his fellow southern mayors: the city that reached its victory bond quota first would host the other mayors. Birmingham at that point was leading, and Hartsfield remarked, "frankly I don't want to go to Birmingham to eat crow." He paused. "As a matter of fact," he said, "I just plain don't want to go to Birmingham at all."

THE FIRST HUNDRED YEARS

THE YEAR 1948 marked Atlanta's one hundredth anniversary as an organized municipality, and Hartsfield, with his showman's instinct, did not let this pass unnoticed. After conferring with Margaret Mitchell, his advisor on matters of history, he dug into the ancient files at City Hall, found there the minutes of the first meeting of city council, held on Wednesday, February 2, 1848, and had copies made for preservation at the Atlanta Historical Society. John Ashley Jones, Walter McElreath, Franklin Garrett, Stephens Mitchell, and others interested in dramatizing the centennial used these documents to script a reenactment of this meeting, which was held at Wesley Memorial Church on February 2, 1948. Great-grandsons or great-nephews of many of the original city officials appeared in a tableau of this first meeting, dressed in costumes of the age. John Ashley Jones, as narrator, described what had gone on before 1848, when the little city was called Terminus, and gave his vision of the future. Franklin Garrett traced the family histories of those in the tableau. Hartsfield and his council were special guests, with the mayor giving *his* version of Atlanta's destiny—which naturally touched strongly upon the need for expansion far beyond the current distance from the zero mile post.

The day before, at the morning service of Druid Hills Baptist Church, Hartsfield had given a talk covering Atlanta's history from its beginning. Three little churches—the Baptist, the Methodist and the Presbyterian—were organized within thirty days of the city's founding, he pointed out, and Atlantans had been a churchgoing people ever since. Mayor Formwalt and his councilmen were very harsh on the lawless element in the little frontier town, and on the night of his election there was a street confrontation between the good citizens and the rowdies which resulted in the roughnecks being run out of town. Indirectly making the point that he, too, had come to the mayor's chair on a law-and-order campaign, Hartsfield reminded his listeners that throughout Atlanta's history, "whenever control of the city was threatened by the wrong element, our good citizens have always measured up to their high ideals of the past and put the town back upon the course of decency and honor. May it always be that way in the future."

"From that little muddy village of some 1,000 valiant souls," said Hartsfield in closing, "we are today the twenty-eighth city of the nation, with 350,000 people inside our limits and 595,000 more in our metropolitan area. And these are those who predict that our real growth has just begun. But as we go into another hundred years of progress let us all hope and pray that ours will always be a city of God-fearing men and women who put character and principle above mere gain . . . a city where families may prosper and little children laugh and play—a city whose people are proud in the knowledge that they live in the atmosphere of decency, honor, and good citizenship."[1]

Another highlight of Atlanta's one hundredth year, for Hartsfield, was the day when Margaret Mitchell came to City Hall, and with councilmen and aldermen standing by, cut the city's birthday cake and gave the first slice to the mayor.

The year marked another anniversary that Hartsfield was happy to have his city observe officially. His friend and stout supporter Robert Woodruff was marking his twenty-fifth anniversary as head of The Coca-Cola Company either as president or chairman of the board. Under his leadership the company had earned an international reputation not only for efficient management but for the intangible qualities of good citizenship, fair trade practices, and general good will, to a degree unexcelled in American business. This was a great credit to Atlanta, the birthplace of Woodruff's great company, Hartsfield said. Therefore, it was resolved that the mayor and the city council would extend the official congratulations of the city of Atlanta to Woodruff for his twenty-five years of brilliant service to his company and to his home community, and they joined with his business colleagues in the hope that he would be spared for many more years of fruitful service.[2]

Several events occurring in 1948 might well be looked upon as landmarks to be remembered a hundred years hence. One was the formal merger of Atlanta's black Democrats, under A. T. Walden, and black Republicans, under John Wesley Dobbs, into the organization called the Negro Voters' League. These were the black leaders who screened white candidates for office, passed their names on to the mass of the black electorate, and by eliminating those most hostile to the black cause set in motion the slow drift toward racial understanding that kept the town relatively at peace. Outside political observers gave Hartsfield credit for working out the delicate balance of this relationship by which the Negroes made enough progress to keep them quiet for the moment, while not moving so fast as to stir up the violent anti-Negro element. Hartsfield would be the last to deny that in his long tenure as mayor, he, more than any other public figure, shaped the city's race relations. Shortly after he left office he was heard to say, privately, that he knew how to "use" the Negro, but was able successfully to avoid letting the Negro "use" him.

Another proud moment for Hartsfield came in May 1948 when an expanded air terminal was dedicated, a concourse of new buildings which added to the comfort of airport visitors as well as airline passengers. Hartsfield's primary interest had always been in lights, towers, longer and stronger runways, but he could make the proud assertion at the dedication ceremonies that "now Atlanta can treat a passenger like a king on the ground."[3] The terminal dedication, which under Helen Bullard's management took on the atmosphere of a huge cocktail party with wine flowing freely, was quickly followed by the inaugural flight of Capitol Airlines into Atlanta. Such progress Hartsfield was determined would be continued. But first there were certain essential things that had to be done.

He had gone into the postwar years determined to dismantle the city government structure and reshape it nearer to his heart's desire. The government, he felt, should be "modernized and streamlined to fit in with present day problems and opportunities." The old-fashioned system of administration under which Atlanta operated was "redolent with the smell of lavender and old lace, of gas lights and the horse and buggy."[4] If a pioneer Atlantan should rise from his grave in Oakland Cemetery and walk through the city, he would be astonished at its tremendous growth and modernity. Only in City Hall would he feel at home, for there he would find the same old form of city government in effect since Atlanta was in swaddling clothes.

There was no real administrative head to the city of Atlanta. The mayor was powerless, except for what influence he could exert on council by the sheer force of his personality. As for the city council, it was the only effective legal head of government, but, said Hartsfield, it represented a system by which "everyone can escape individual responsibility while the people must grope around trying to find out who is legally responsible for what."

The council, he said, would do a great service to Atlanta if it could recommend to the legislature the charter revision set forth by Dr. Thomas H. Read's report which had been gathering dust for nine years. This report called for an executive head to whom all departments would be responsible and who would exercise constant and minute supervision over everything that was going on in government. This was the point which appealed to Hartsfield, for it would allow him to do something about the petty politicians, drones, and do-nothings who, under the current system, were thwarting progress and perpetuating inequities. Then came the matter closest to his heart—corporate expansion. Most postwar industrial growth, he said, would take place outside the city limits. Atlanta would be called upon to support this expansion. Consequently, Atlanta could not be denied the right to expand its corporate limits to take in the areas on its boundaries which it would be called on to support with water, sewage, and other city services. He returned to the theme in his address to council a year later, as he reviewed the accomplishments of 1946: "Our inside citizens are going to be very sensitive about . . . incurring other financial obligations benefiting any areas adjacent to our limits which areas themselves are unwilling to assume the common burdens of city maintenance."[5]

There was little chance, Hartsfield indicated, that adjoining local governments would welcome being brought into the city until a charter revision had gotten rid of the multiplicity of functions and divisions of authority under which the city now functioned. So long as this condition prevailed, other governments in the metro area would have no respect for Atlanta and would ever look upon its government with outright hostility.

In the next five years, he argued, corporate Atlanta was going forward as never before—or it was going to fall back. Opportunity was knocking. Business and industry were looking toward Atlanta. Thousands of new citizens were moving into the area. Improvement and progress are in the air, he told council. "Let us therefore swing the government of Atlanta into line with the inevitable destiny of a great Southern city."[6]

Hartsfield's arguments for progress had not gone unheeded. In 1946 the city had voted a $20.4 million bond issue for a multitude of improvements. Half expecting to have jobless veterans hungrily walking its streets selling pencils, victims of a postwar depression, Atlanta instead found work aplenty and labor scarce as more than 250 new industries moved in after the war. Prices went sky high and there was an acute shortage of housing. In the first years after the war certain weaknesses in city services were demonstrated too. Early on the morning of December 7, 1946, 119 persons died in a fire at the Winecoff Hotel. Building construction, fire equipment, and firemen's training all proved completely inadequate as the victims, many of them young boys and girls in town for a YMCA meeting, died in the flames or by suffocation, or by leaping from high windows to the pavements. It was the world's worst hotel fire up to that time. Hartsfield, terribly saddened and distressed, moved immediately to establish a committee of professional engineers to lay down rules for construction and remodeling of high-rise buildings which would make such holocausts impossible in the future.

Hartsfield's deepest thoughts were always upon the question of annexation. Atlanta in 1948 was only thirty-five square miles, which made it fiftieth in the nation in land area, but with an estimated 350,000 people inside these boundaries, it was thirty-second in population. Around it in East Point, Hapeville, College Park, and Decatur, and in such unincorporated areas as Buckhead, there were 595,000 more. Twice his efforts to annex Buckhead had failed—and twice he had growled ominously that this was ridiculous, for if there were no Atlanta, there would be no affluent north side. The moving of young, vigorous, active people into the suburbs, Hartsfield argued, would cause the city to suffer in several ways. It left the inner city vulnerable to the criminal and to the machine politician. And it left all citizens subject to higher taxes; for, he pointed out, Fulton

County would have to levy a higher impost on both inner-city and county residents to give them sewers and water and streets, fire and police protection. By now Hartsfield was getting support from some prominent citizens who shared his view that Atlanta must break out of its political straitjacket. Stephens Mitchell led them as chairman of a group calling itself the Committee for Greater Atlanta.

Hartsfield had hoped that in its centennial year Atlanta would at last expand its city limits. Again, it was not to be. No matter how hard he struck out at legislators controlled by courthouse politicians and selfish Buckhead merchants, for a third time the expansion effort failed.

The next year was an election year and again Hartsfield won after a tough name-calling battle, defeating his old enemy Charlie Brown by some 3,000 votes, though his majority over his other two opponents and Brown combined was only 102 votes. As usual there were charges that the voting machines had been tampered with, and as usual there was a whispering campaign to the effect that Hartsfield was a man with a roving eye where pretty women were concerned. Anonymous telephone calls conveying this message went to prominent Baptist ministers around town, but Hartsfield was not dismayed. He explained to his preacher friends that they came from a psychopathic ex-policeman who had been making such charges for years. The Hartsfield-as-Lothario issue did not seem to have much effect on the electorate, but his opposition to unionizing the police and his protests against a streetcar operators' strike did bring a confrontation with some labor leaders, and his support of rent controls and public housing contributed to his near defeat. Letters from Senator G. Everett Millican kept pleading, "whatever you do, don't jump on organized labor." Millican was not the only one who sought to guide him. A Catholic journalist, Mary E. Campbell, wrote, "You, like our Lord, are being unjustly condemned for things you have no jurisdiction over, and a lot of harm is being done by rumors that you are against our faith."[7] She then sent him a beautiful prayer, which she hoped he would say before the crucifix over the main altar at Sacred Heart Church, and some excerpts from a speech by Cardinal Francis Spellman, which she suggested Hartsfield incorporate in his radio talks. It would allay any rumors that he was anti-Catholic, she said.

A letter he received from Helen Bullard at the end of the race cheered him immeasurably. Speaking on behalf of Charles A. Rawson and Associates, she said, "In the past eight years we have handled twenty-one political campaigns but we never handled one that gave us as much satisfaction as yours. Your complete cooperation made working with you a joy . . . We send you our unbounded admiration."[8] Hartsfield could have written a letter of equally heartfelt thanks to Miss Bullard, whose uncanny political sense was to guide him, and his successor Ivan Allen, for years.

Another letter, from Jake Carlton the former *Journal* reporter, also gave Hartsfield a warm glow. Writing from Washington, Carlton said: "It may be of some consolation to you to know that for years I have told people you were one of the few people in politics I have 'covered' who seemed to me absolutely honest. As far as I know you never told a reporter a lie, nor engaged in the so-popular political sport of four-flushing. Over the years that has been good politics, I think."[9]

What Carlton did not know, nor did many others in Atlanta, was that Hartsfield early in 1949 was ready to give up his mayor's job and go on to higher things. He had spent a number of days in early March in the hospital, recovering from a severe sinus infection, and he had time to do some thinking. By mid-April he was writing to his good friend Jimmy Dobbs, of the Dobbs House chain, in Memphis:

[This is] in great confidence, so far as Atlanta is concerned. The office of Assistant Secretary of Commerce for Aeronautics is open. It is the boss of Civil Aviation in America, the head of CAA, the U.S. Coast and Geodetic Survey and the Weather Bureau.

Some of my friends in Washington, mostly among the U.S. Mayors' Conference have mentioned me for the place. They feel that on account of my twenty-five years of intimate contact with civil aviation, that I would be qualified for the job. Also that having been Mayor of a large city for eleven years, that also answers a lot of questions.

As you know this is a political year in Atlanta, and confidentially I am just surfeited with local honors. I have accomplished a lot and am just full up. Incidentally the town is in good shape and politically I am on top. I can get re-elected; but what then? Just another four years of back-breaking work, and so far as a good record is concerned, just betting against myself.

Cooper Green of Birmingham was elected the new President of the U.S. Conference of Mayors and he is rooting for me in Washington. He has gotten several other Mayors to go to the bat, on the score that cities want a man in charge who knows their problems . . . on civil aviation and airport work.

The salary is about the same as here, so it is nothing but the honor for the next three and one half years. The place is filled by the President [Truman], and cleared through Mr. Wm. Boyle, Asst. to the Chairman of the Democratic National Committee. The new assistant has also to be agreeable with Secretary of Commerce Charles Sawyer. In other words, these three will dictate the matter. Cooper has wired the President and Wm. Boyle and also the Mayors of Jacksonville, Chattanooga, Charlotte and Columbia, S.C. My entire State delegation in Congress is also for me.

If you know any other Democratic Mayors or public officials in other States who might be willing to help me, it would surely be appreciated. Since the matter can be decided at any time, telegrams to the President, Mr. Wm. Boyle of the National Democratic Committee are necessary.

How about some of your friends in Tennessee? If your Mayor would do this, it would be appreciated, as well as any other Tennessee Democratic mayors, or Senators, or Congressmen.

I can't afford to let any local officials know about this as it would foul me up locally, to be put in the position of stepping out, and I might change my mind, if this does not materialize. However, I am told that I am right up in the running with the best chance of all. If you contact me, let it be in riddles if by telegraph, or write me at my Grant Building office c/o Miss Bettis who always knows more about myself than I do.[10]

Dobbs, an Atlanta airport concessionaire, did all he could to help. He wrote a personal letter to President Truman, with whom he had once played poker, sending him a resumé of Hartsfield's achievements in aviation. He wrote to Senator K. D. McKellar and Representative Clifford Davis of Tennessee, telling them he had never known a finer man nor a cleaner one than Bill Hartsfield. Robert Woodruff wrote to Charles Sawyer, secretary of commerce; and Chip Robert, still a power in Washington politics, pushed for Hartsfield through William Boyle, Jr., whose recommendation, presumably, Truman would take. Senator Walter F. George, James C. Davis, and Congressman Carl Vinson all put in a word for Hartsfield.

All seemed rosy at first, but as spring wore on and June drew near, when Hartsfield would have to make up his mind whether to run again for mayor in September, the feedback from Washington remained noncommittal. Hartsfield began to get a little nervous. Then, on May 6, Robert Ramspeck, executive vice-president of the Air Transport Association of America and former congressman, wrote Hartsfield to tell him that the word around Washington was that Secretary Sawyer felt that he did not really need an assistant secretary for air. About the same time a little notice appeared in the *American Aviation Daily.* It said that the position of assistant secretary of commerce for air probably would not be filled for a while.

Hartsfield turned this over in his mind. The federal salary would be less than he was making as mayor. Mrs. Hartsfield, he knew, hated Washington and would not be happy there. And there was Cousin Claude's health and welfare to worry about, and his many mining interests in Georgia still occupied his mind. All at once the job he knew best, and handled so well, seemed highly desirable once more. He announced for mayor, and in early June immediately launched the kind of knife-fighting campaign he so much enjoyed.

Little else gave him pleasure in that busy year, except his victory in the mayor's race. One morning in August the dreadful word came to him that Margaret Mitchell, after a gallant five-day fight, had died of injuries suffered when she had been struck by a speeding taxi on Peachtree Street. On the back of a letter that had just come in, he began slowly to put down, in a trembling hand, his tribute to her. "I have lost one of my closest personal friends, and Atlanta has lost her greatest and finest citizen." On August 28, twelve days after her death, a letter came to Hartsfield from Stephens Mitchell, her brother: "I want to thank you for your kindness during the recent tragedy in our family, and to tell you that every employee of the city with whom we came in contact was courteous and kind, efficient and sympathetic." He had especially high praise for Frank Wilson, superintendent of Grady Hospital, whose staff had fought so gallantly to save his little sister, and for Chief Jenkins, whose motorcycle police had guided her cortege through ranks of mourning thousands, from Spring Hill to Oakland Cemetery. Miss Mitchell had been struck down on the evening of August 11, and his political opponents, naturally, blamed Hartsfield for letting a cab driver with an accident-prone background roam the streets. The next day, heavy of heart, he experienced what under different circumstances would have been a proudly triumphant moment. With the election less than a month away, Plaza Park, a tiny postage stamp of greenery over the smoky chasm of the old railroad gulch, was dedicated. Hartsfield told those who came to the dedication that for more than fifty years Atlantans who had a feeling for beauty had wanted to cover over the railroad tracks that split the heart of downtown in two. At last the first step had been taken. One block had been cov-

ered, trees planted, grass sown, a fountain set in play. As Hartsfield talked, a plane trailing a banner advertising the candidacy
of one of his opponents flew over. Hartsfield seemed to welcome the interruption. "Look up in the air and see promises,"
he said. "Then look down here with me and see performance."[11]

His opponent had charged Hartsfield with wasting the people's money on the park—a sensitive point with a man who
prided himself on watching every civic nickel. The total cost,
he said, was less than half a million dollars, and this was seventy-five thousand dollars less than the original engineering
estimate. And instead of being something rammed down the
people's throats, as his opponent charged, it had been specifically approved in 1946, in the $20.4 million bond issue that
provided the funds. It also had the approval of the state legislature and the Fulton County Commission. And it would not
only add badly needed beauty to a rundown section, it would
pay for itself, in increased taxes on the land around it, inside
ten years, he argued. His opponents predicted the park would
become what it later did become, a hangout for winos and
moochers. Not so, said Hartsfield. It would be a place of rest,
which would serve "thousands of tired women with children,
worn out with shopping, old people and pensioners, and those
who are on a split shift or a five day week—people who have a
perfect right to be downtown, but who have no place to sit
down or get a drink of water."[12] Critics pointed out that tired
mothers with children often found themselves in more desperate need of a toilet than of a drinking fountain. Hartsfield admitted this was true, but restrooms, he pointed out, attracted
all sorts of folks and could not be made part of a park as small
as this.

Another triumphant moment came in this election year when
his alma mater, the downtown public library on Carnegie Way,
was completely remodeled, another project financed by the
1946 bond issue. Remembering the days he had spent in the

stacks, educating himself after quitting high school, he took great pride in the library and would fiercely denounce anybody who tried to tell him that libraries in other cities were also doing creative and innovative things. To him no library in the country was as good as the Atlanta library, and he intended to keep it that way. He had no patience with adults who did not continue their education by reading, and he believed strongly that once a young adult experienced the joy of reading he would never be the same again. He also had a hangup about librarians who wanted to see all their books on the shelves. He once said that his happiest day would be when he would walk into the library and find all the shelves empty, with every book checked out and being read.

Weary as he might be of the arduous job of mayor, and tired of the empty honors it brought, Hartsfield at the end of this election year could look back over his career with a certain satisfaction. He remembered the naive young man making his first race for alderman in 1923, passing out his cards, shaking hands right and left, flashing a gleaming ear-to-ear smile. He remembered with a chuckle now an event in one of those early campaigns that had left him crimson with embarrassment. Headed for a political rally in a private home in an unfamiliar neighborhood, he saw a crowd gathering in a yard. He went up and started smiling and grabbing hands and passing out his cards. But nobody smiled back. And suddenly it dawned on him that he was at the wrong house. He was electioneering in a crowd that was gathering for a funeral.

AT LAST THE CHAINS ARE BROKEN

HARTSFIELD STEPPED FEISTILY into the 1950s with his hat cocked jauntily over one ear. The year just past, he told his councilmen, was one of the greatest in Atlanta's history so far as improvements were concerned. There had been progress across the board for all of Atlanta's citizens. Branch libraries and parks had been built, sewers and streets laid down, and further improvements were on the drawing board to be completed in 1950. The expressway system was well under way, and when it was completed it would constitute "one of the most ambitious highway and traffic improvement programs ever undertaken by an American city."[1] The airport, his first love, was doing particularly well. New and larger runways had been completed and further extensions were in progress. To a frugal man like Hartsfield it was particularly pleasing that the airport was more than paying its way. It required ninety-five thousand dollars in operating funds, but it was taking in more than two hundred thousand dollars in landing fees and ground rents. "I think," he said, "when the final history of our city is made the years 1948, 1949, and 1950 will stand out as a period of Atlanta's greatest progress."[2]

In 1950 Hartsfield realized an ambition that long had eluded him. On his birthday, March 1, he and his good friend Chip Robert set off for Europe, ostensibly to inspect Scandinavian garbage incinerators, which Hartsfield favored for use in Atlanta. The pictures they sent back, however, indicated that Hartsfield, at least, was the incorrigible tourist, keeping his little hand-held movie camera whirring. Somewhat to Hartsfield's chagrin, Chip Robert attracted the greatest attention, for he was using a Polaroid camera, a new thing in Europe.

Word that Hartsfield was going to Europe set wheels turning in both Washington and Atlanta. Joe Jones, right-hand man to Robert Woodruff, got off word to Coca-Cola people in London, Paris, Rome, Berlin, Stockholm, and Copenhagen, telling them to give the mayor and Chip Robert the big hello. Dick Rich, of Rich's, got in touch with his business connections in the major capitals, and Hartsfield was practically hand-carried wherever he went. Many of the Coca-Cola people in Europe already knew Hartsfield, for when they visited the U.S.A. he, like the Cyclorama and Stone Mountain, was a sight to be seen in Atlanta. He would welcome them to his office and pose them in front of a large portrait of Woodruff.

Hartsfield, while in England, learned that the French communists were trying to banish Coke from France on the false charge that it was deleterious to the health. Hartsfield suggested that he fly over to Paris carrying several cases of Coca-Cola, which he would drink on all public occasions. The French could look upon him and see that he was still in glowing health after a lifetime of drinking Coke. The Coca-Cola people in London dissuaded him, for they were at the moment in delicate negotiations with the French government. In Rome the local mayor had himself photographed drinking an authentic Coke, a bold gesture politically, for the communists were also attacking Coke sales in Italy.

Hartsfield's loyalty to the Scripto ball-point pen, made in Atlanta by his friend James H. Carmichael, was equal to his loyalty to Coca-Cola, and he carried dozens of these, giving them away to everybody from taxi drivers to chief magistrates, all over Europe. He was amazed at the good will they created.

Hartsfield was particularly anxious to make a side trip to Berlin to call on Mayor Ernst Reuter, who a year earlier had visited him in Atlanta. (Hartsfield had driven him out to see the home of General Lucius Clay, the NATO commander.) Hartsfield's request to Senator Walter George to do a little gentle prodding of the State Department and the Department of Defense quickly cleared away all obstacles, and Hartsfield—who had been turned down earlier when he had asked that American mayors be invited to Germany to see the death camps—made his visit to Berlin under the wing of the military. They were made welcome by Mayor Reuter, but when they went sightseeing and stopped by the Brandenburg Gate, the Russian sentries guarding the entrance to the Soviet sector made them feel less welcome. When Chip Robert took a Polaroid picture of a sentry and offered it to him, he refused it, and when Hartsfield started taking movies of two old women cleaning rubble in the Russian sector, one turned her backside toward him and the other, waving her arms wildly, demanded that he leave her alone.

Hartsfield recalled this as his only rebuke in Europe. Everywhere else, when his name was introduced, the listener's face lighted up—associating him with Atlanta, the city of *Gone with the Wind*. To Hartsfield, instinctively a showman, this seemed to be a situation that should be exploited. Shortly after he returned home he wrote Arthur Loew of Loew's, Incorporated, telling him of the tremendous interest in *Gone with the Wind* and offering to use what influence he had in the United States to have the picture shown in Germany. The book was very popular in Germany, he pointed out, for the Germans, in the destruction their city had suffered, felt a kinship to the Atlantans who had survived the Civil War. Admitting that the idea stemmed from the fact that he was at heart a showman, he told Loew that he had made some friends in Berlin among the army authorities and in the city government itself, and he stood ready to help in any way he could to arrange a special showing in Berlin, which he was sure would be given worldwide publicity. Loew had had the same thoughts even earlier. A note from one of his assistants to Hartsfield told the mayor that at that moment the picture's dialogue was being synchronized in German and *Gone with the Wind* would be released in Germany sometime in 1951.

Hartsfield's first trip abroad lingered long in his memory, and for weeks after his return he showed his and Chip's pictures and regaled all who would listen with his observations. The sentry who refused the picture Chip Robert offered, the old women angry at him for taking their picture were significant events to him. They portrayed the deep distrust of the Russians for the West. As for the feeling of the West toward the Russians, everywhere he went—London, Paris, Rome, Stockholm, Copenhagen, or Berlin—there was a deep-seated terror of the Soviet Union. The utter destruction of Berlin was the most impressive thing he saw on his whole trip, he said. It was like driving from Atlanta's airport to Buckhead and seeing the whole city flattened. And when he talked to the Berliners' city government at the Rathaus (city hall) he told them, with deep and genuine emotion, how he admired their courage in fighting for democracy in the shadow of communist Russia. The wall was not yet up, and he went into bookstores in the Russian sector and bought huge, and handsomely printed, Russian propaganda posters, extolling communism and denouncing capitalism.

In contrast to the Allied sector of Berlin, Hartsfield found London to be a tired old woman sitting in her house surrounded by the relics of her past. The British, he felt, had lost their historic initiative once the Empire was lost, and now, instead of buckling down to work, the people were trying to vote themselves into prosperity by opting for shorter hours, more benefits, larger pensions. To Hartsfield, a "workaholic", this meant trouble in the future.

Never one to conceal his thoughts and feelings, Hartsfield listened a moment to the debaters in Hyde Park—two cockneys arguing some abstruse point of metaphysics—and then jumped in himself with some observations about the relative merits of the free enterprise system and the socialist state. He was doing very well in his defense of the American way until his British opponents asked him how he reconciled his concepts of free enterprise with the high protective tariffs the American government imposed, thus shutting European manufacturers out of American markets. At this Hartsfield took evasive action with the professional politician's old verbal feint: "Oh, I'm all right on that," he said. He then flipped his wide-brimmed hat down over one eye, adjusted the lapels of his double-breasted gray flannel suit, and strolled off to photograph the changing of the guard at Buckingham Palace.

Paris he found to be beautiful and different, and he spent much of his time there photographing the zoo, gathering ideas for improving the zoo at home. In Paris he found labor unsettled. The taxi drivers and the airline porters both went on strike while he was there, leaving him to carry his own bags. Out of an instinctive sympathy for the city worker he took the inconvenience calmly, for he learned that most Parisian workers did have real grievances. In France he discovered it was the farmers who were the politically favored group. Rome he remembered with regret, for there his movie camera went on the blink at a crucial moment—as he was photographing a vast Holy Year throng in Saint Peter's Square.

In each town Hartsfield and Robert were welcomed at the city hall and given the honors due a mayor. Hartsfield, never at loss, handled himself with great aplomb, except on one formal occasion in Stockholm. Hartsfield was not much of a drinking man, and the Scandinavians have a custom of drinking toasts in Aquavit, a fiery liqueur, in tiny glasses; and in the interludes between the formal toasts, in which all "Skoal" together, individual diners look about the table and catch another diner's eye, each lifts his glass, says "Skoal," and drinks a private toast. One evening, after skoaling and being skoaled by some thirty other guests, Hartsfield had to be carried out. He also quickly discovered what Chip Robert long before had learned from such far-traveling friends as Mayor John S. Cohen—that the quickest way to gain working knowledge of a foreign language is through the help of a "pillow dictionary." Word of this tutoring evidently followed him home. Later, when foreign officials he had met on his trip wrote him letters in their language, he would give them to Miss Ira Jarrell, superintendent of schools, to translate. This she did happily enough, though adding that when he received letters from the "mesdemoiselles de la boulevard" he had undoubtedly met, she would be happy to translate those too.

Hartsfield came home from Europe to face the same labor troubles that had plagued him the year before. In May 1949 the bus and trackless-trolley drivers had gone on a nineteen-day strike, despite Hartsfield's earnest pleas that they keep the buses running while they argued over the issues. A year later, on March 18, they struck again, to the great distress of the trolley-riding public. The drivers who had walked off the buses went on the streets in their own cars, hauling passengers "free" —or for whatever gratuity the rider might wish to give them. This led to misunderstandings, and the city's solution was to revive the old system of jitneys, banned from Atlanta streets for twenty-five years. These were privately owned vehicles, licensed by the city and permitted to charge a ten-cent fare. When, after thirty-seven days, the strikers went back to work on June 24, 1950 they were no longer employees of the public utility, the Georgia Power Company. They drove under the banner of the Atlanta Transit Company, a privately owned firm made up largely of bankers and lawyers.

Two days after the trolley strike was settled, Hartsfield had matters of even greater moment to concern him. The North Koreans attacked across the thirty-eighth parallel. Atlanta, like the rest of the nation, faced another long drawn-out and bloody war. Hartsfield, with a world war just five years behind him, knew what this meant—shortages, both in materials and manpower.

For Hartsfield, for Atlanta, and for Fulton and DeKalb counties, 1951 was a landmark year. To Hartsfield, what he called "suburbanitis" was the great enemy of a city's progress, and ever since he had been in office he had argued with great eloquence for the annexation to the city of the burgeoning suburbs, particularly those in the northwest section where a great postwar boom in housing had taken place, filling up unincorporated areas of Fulton and DeKalb counties with the affluent, educated, and ambitious citizens who made their living in Atlanta but left its government to others. In 1947 a referendum had failed, and Hartsfield, changing tactics, had sought to send to the Georgia legislature representatives who shared his views on city-county consolidated services and the annexation of Buckhead and Cascade Heights. In 1950 a local government commission, composed of supposedly disinterested and unbiased citizens, was appointed to study the subject and make recommendations on which the legislature could act. The strategy worked. The word "annexation" was dropped, and a slate of legislators, pledged to what some public-relations genius had renamed the "Plan of Improvement," was elected. And in 1951, to Hartsfield's vast relief, this fabulous realignment was voted into law, to take effect on January 1, 1952. Based on the old Read Report, moribund since 1938, the Plan of Improvement was the most innovative change in Atlanta's municipal government in half a century. It eliminated costly duplication of city and county services. The city was to furnish parks and fire and police services; the county would look after matters of health and welfare, assessing and collecting taxes for both governmental units. All functions of the two governments, so often competitive and squabbling in the past, would be coordinated, except the school systems, which would remain separate.

As satisfying to Hartsfield as the realignment of functions was the element of expansion. His domain had tripled in size, to 118 square miles, and some hundred thousand new citizens had come under his benign jurisdiction. Albert Riley, in the *Journal* and *Constitution* of January 1, 1952, reflected in his prose the warm glow of pride and happiness that the mayor felt. "In one great stride," said Riley, "the city broke the rusty chains of corporate limits that had restricted its growth for twenty years. It was one of the really great moments in Atlanta's history, comparable almost to the city's rising from the smoldering ashes Sherman left behind him in 1864."

While Hartsfield on January 7, 1951 was nursing through the legislature the bill under which the Plan of Improvement would come into being, he was typically thinking far into the future, laying plans by which a city so vastly expanded in size and population could meet its new responsibilities. Still of great concern to him was the development of the Chattahoochee River system, to insure an adequate supply of water for generations to come. The key to this development was the construction of Buford Dam, a forty-million-dollar project of the Corps of Engineers. The dam had been approved and more than two million dollars had been spent on preliminary construction when in June 1951 the House Committee on Appropriations refused to recommend that additional money be spent. To Hartsfield this was incredible. Buford Dam meant that electricity could be generated for the multitude of industries which he foresaw coming into the Southeast in the future. It would control the flow of the river for navigation purposes; it would offer recreation to thousands of Georgians who would love to fish and swim and sail on blue waters under clear skies, pushed by clean cool winds. Throughout the summer he traveled back and forth to Washington, calling on Senators George and Russell and the Georgia delegates, repeating the old refrain. The dam must be built. Water is the key to civilization. In his annual address to council he pulled out all the stops. He recalled the great drought of 1925, which if repeated would cause Atlanta to ration its water and would close down the power plants that took vast amounts of cooling water from the stream.

I earnestly beg and plead with our newspapers, and all of their news and editorial writers, and with all civic and industrial groups and patriotic citizens of metropolitan Atlanta, to inform themselves upon this matter of future water supply upon which the very life or death of our community depends. When they do, they will realize it is the most important fact in our future, as well as in the national defense, so far as the Atlanta area is concerned . . . I call upon these and all good citizens to join in seeing that the Buford dam is completed.[3]

And finally, of course, it was, with Hartsfield, smiling proudly, looming large among the dignitaries, smugly conscious of the fact that he, as much as any man, was responsible for the great work and all the good that would proceed from it.

The year 1951 brought one moment of political tension. Hartsfield, it must be remembered, had once looked with strong suspicion upon the activities of the NAACP and had asked friends in Washington to try to discover the sources of its income, which he suspected might stem from subversive elements. By 1951 this attitude seems to have been modified considerably. The NAACP held its national convention in Atlanta in July 1951, and Hartsfield welcomed it as warmly as if it had been a meeting of the National Association of Manufacturers. He told the mixed audience that he was happy to have people come here from all over the nation to see for themselves the marvelous progress being made in Atlanta and the deep South. The South in the past had been a neglected impoverished section, and many of the region's deficiencies in public service and in education were due solely to the fact that there was no money to do the things that should have been done. This situation, however, was changing, with federal aid giving the poorer regions a fairer share of the national income, with better educational opportunities, and with increasing industrialization. The South, and particularly the Atlanta area, was beginning to move forward as never before. And the citizens the NAACP represented were beginning to share in that progress.

He then paid tribute to the Negro citizens of Atlanta, to the black newspaper publishers, bankers, insurance men, merchants, and professional men who formed an important part of the civic and commercial life of the city:

Here in our own city government we are proud of the progress that is being made in amicable race relations. We have and are making progress in increased public housing for our Negro citizens. We have built new parks and libraries; we have aided in the development of new residential subdivisions; we have greatly increased our public health appropriations and the health service rendered to Negro citizens. In the field of hospitals, our Hospital Authority is even now bringing to completion a great new Negro hospital for the use of those not classed as charity cases.

In the field of common schools we are spending millions in the erection of modern schools of the very highest quality. As evidence of that progress, in 1944 there were only 178 Negro teachers, teaching 20,000 children, while today there are 700 teachers teaching the same number of our Negro children. Since 1945 we have added 180 class rooms to schools used by our Negro patrons as well as new auditoriums, cafeterias, libraries, gymnasiums, etc. Incidentally, our Negro high schools are accredited with an A rating by the Southeastern Association of Schools and Colleges.

While here in Atlanta we invite you to see and inspect some of the residential subdivisions where our Negro citizens of increasing incomes have built beautiful homes. Likewise we hope you will look over the great Carver Vocational Educational School run by Atlanta and Fulton County jointly for our Negro citizens.

Truly, my friends, the record in Atlanta has been one of great and continued progress, under a city administration which believes in fairness and justice for all of our citizens.

Such a city, my friends, and such a people, welcome you to Atlanta. We hope you will look us over thoroughly with kindly and understanding hearts and minds, observe the progress that is being made, and go away with a happy and pleasant impression of our great and friendly City of Atlanta.

The city government formally bids your convention welcome to Atlanta.[4]

Hartsfield's handling of the NAACP welcome brought applause from the *Atlanta Constitution*, which said that his action brought good national and international publicity to the city. Only the Russians, the *Constitution* said, were disappointed.

They had hoped the Ku Klux Klan would demonstrate, and there would be some police action against the city. Imagine what a field day the Communists would have had if there had been trouble. Atlanta and Georgia's name would have been dragged over all the world as places of violence and of the denial of the justice and rights which we boast for all our people. But he did a good job. The NAACP met, advanced its proposals, with which many people do not entirely agree, enjoyed the guarantees of free speech and assembly and departed . . . We think the mayor, the city officials, the police and the city itself deserve the hearty congratulations of all thoughtful citizens.[5]

Not all Atlanta citizens held this view. There was a flurry of protest immediately after the convention, and two months later reprints of a *Pittsburgh Courier* front page were being widely circulated. The paper pictured Hartsfield sitting on the platform with the NAACP leaders and showed whites and blacks dancing together. The captions said this was taking place "just two blocks away from Governor Herman Talmadge's capital," and "the statue of 'Gene' Talmadge didn't even turn around."[6]

From Chief Luther Spinks of the Decatur Police Department Hartsfield received a copy of "this regrettable piece of Communist Slander" along with a note assuring the mayor that if Spinks caught anybody distributing literature of this nature, "it will be destroyed with a strong reprimand. As a person who holds a Political job I understand there are people who would stoop to such ridiculous things to persecute you."[7] Hartsfield wrote back his thanks and told Spinks that some ten thousand of these flyers had been put out by a Klan official, who had them printed in Augusta. They were being circulated over the state by the county-unit advocates as part of the argument that Atlanta Negroes would dominate the state unless the county-unit system was retained. Naturally, he added, "what few Communist agitators we have make full use of this situation in trying to stir up racial troubles." Those who circulate this kind of literature would bear watching, he said, for "they will be the ones behind any future outbreaks which may occur." His political enemies, hopeful of being mayor themselves, also liked to see these circulars scattered around. And in response to the criticism of his welcoming speech, Hartsfield remarked, "Mayors have been greeting conventions of Baptists, Catholics, Jews, white and colored for many years without being accused of being a part of that which they greet."

Though the Supreme Court decision that would outlaw the county-unit system was still ten years away, Hartsfield and Atlanta already were identified in the minds of rural Georgians with the attack on its inequities. Hartsfield's welcome to the NAACP was a warning to rural Georgia that only the countervailing weight of the small-county vote could save the state from big-city rule.

In April 1951 Hartsfield made his annual pilgrimage to New Orleans, driving cross-country with Police Lieutenant Charles Cook at the wheel, and two city hall reporters, John Crown of the *Journal* and Herman Hancock of the *Constitution*. Also along was banker Ralph Huie, chairman of the finance committee of city council. His purpose was, as in the past, to call upon

Cooper Green in Birmingham and deLesseps Morrison in New Orleans, to find out how their cities were faring and to learn, if possible, what they might have up their sleeves that Atlanta could emulate—or forestall. Bellingrath Gardens in Mobile was always a stopoff on this journey, and if Hartsfield heard of any mineral, clay, slate, shale, or aggregate, the old prospector in him responded and he drove out of his way to see if the deposit offered any investment possibilities. Though his main interest was in Georgia (he had owned a talc mine operation near Chatsworth for many years), he was constantly on the lookout for opportunities elsewhere. When prospects looked bright he would borrow all he could on his insurance and use whatever money friends might make available. Despite his almost wideeyed faith that some day he would strike it rich in some product of the earth, he had a certain native caution. An Augusta doctor who claimed to have invented a device with which he could find oil and gas fields blindfolded captured his interest at first, but this faded when Garland Peyton, the state geologist, reported that two deposits the doctor said were oil bearing turned out to be dry holes. A promising venture in five small oil wells in Illinois proved to be less profitable than he had hoped, and he was also greatly disturbed at President Truman's efforts to reduce the depletion allowance on talc, clays, and other minerals, in which he had more faith than he did in oil. Such a policy, he argued, would make it impossible for a shoestring speculator such as himself to continue exploration in the earth products.

Back from New Orleans, he set off at once for Bermuda with Chip Robert, going to Tuckerstown and Jackson Dick's place there called "Atlanta by the Sea." Parties given in his honor were attended by assorted Bermuda dignitaries, including the mayors of Hamilton and Saint George's and the Bishop of Bermuda.

Shortly before his journey to Bermuda, his older brother,

Charles Hartsfield, Sr., age sixty-nine, died of a heart ailment at Saint Joseph's hospital. A slender white-haired man who had served for many years as deputy clerk of the criminal division of Fulton Superior Court, Charles had his famous brother's flair for getting along with newspapermen. A gifted raconteur with a sense of history, he loved to tell stories of the Atlanta of his boyhood, and of his little brother Willie. Despite the eight years' difference in their ages, the brothers were very close, and his death was deeply distressing to the mayor.

As the only lawyer in the family, Hartsfield soon found himself helping his brother's children settle their father's estate. This consisted in the main of the house at 300 Milledge Avenue, in which the mayor and his family had lived for many years before moving to Pelham Road. By an agreement worked out by the mayor, Charles Hartsfield, Jr., bought the house from his sister, Mabel, Mrs. Delmar Shelton of Long Beach, California, and his brother John, of Atlanta.

Charles's death and Hartsfield's springtime travels had caused him to miss the Confederate Memorial Day ceremonies at Kingston Cemetery, where he had been asked to deliver the main address, and a letter from Leila Darden told him he was greatly missed. She also notified him that the wall around his mother's family lot was crumbling and must be fixed. Hartsfield, who was a little pressed for cash at the time, wrote back that he of course wanted to keep the lot in shape but he could not afford to spend too much on it. He asked Miss Darden to get him an estimate. Nothing happened until fall, when she wrote him that not only was the wall crumbling but a marker was needed for the grave of his grandfather, Captain Dagnall, the old Seminole Indian fighter. And the repairs on the falling wall would cost $175.

Family problems were overshadowed by a happy advancement at year's end. On December 31, 1951 Hartsfield was elected vice-president of the American Municipal Association, the national organization of mayors—a post that would lead in turn to the presidency of that organization. His friend Aubrey Milam wired his congratulations: "You add prestige to our town and reflect credit on yourself."[8]

Hartsfield began 1952 with two main projects in mind—first, to bring the new areas covered by the Plan of Improvement into the city with as little dislocation as possible; second, to push the expressway system to completion and to build the off-street parking that would clear the downtown streets of the cars the expressways would bring in. Also there had to be some revision of the public transportation system. A city of Atlanta's size could not be served by bus lines running only on one central street. The expansion of the city limits had brought the amphitheater at Chastain Park under city control, and Hartsfield had traveled into North Carolina to see how public amphitheaters were handled there. He came back to assure Atlantans that the theater would be rebuilt, and he would seek city support for the theatrical, musical, and educational programs that would be held there.

The Plan of Improvement has unshackled our town, given it new life and hope. A new spirit of optimism is in the air. True, there are still those who for selfish reasons will try to impede our progress and place obstacles in our path, but we are confident that the great majority of our loyal citizens will approve what we have done, and will support us as long as we honestly and efficiently perform our many and arduous duties in giving to both old and new citizens the many services they deserve as fellow Atlantans.

He ended his address to city council on the familiar bugle note —but this year the call was even more triumphant than usual as he thought of the city, expanded to its true dimensions at last. "Atlanta today, proudly takes her true place among the great cities of the nation. Let us all together make our home town, our Atlanta, the greatest place on earth."[9]

Even as Hartsfield spoke there were some Atlantans who

were determined to carry Atlanta in a direction other than the one he had visualized. The pictures from the *Pittsburgh Courier,* showing Hartsfield sitting beside a Negro woman at the NAACP meeting, were being widely circulated in east Atlanta by a retired captain in the fire department and by a white merchant who ran a small dry-goods store in the Negro section off Boulevard. Hartsfield's informant also told him that he had been in Charlie Brown's office a few days earlier and that Brown, who was planning to announce that he would run for mayor in 1953, did not intend to make his previous mistake and go out for the Negro vote. He was going to hang the black man around Hartsfield's neck, so to speak, and sell himself as the white man's candidate. In early February 1952 Brown did indeed announce that he would run against Hartsfield the following year, and a brief flurry of acrimony made the front pages. Brown described the Hartsfield administration as "a worn out political machine thriving on favoritism," and Hartsfield described Brown as a "candidate of the disgruntled county politicians, the race baiters, and the whole motley crew that oppose all progress and decency in the administration of city affairs." Brown charged Hartsfield with being fifteen years late in building the expressways (the dislike of some legislators for Hartsfield may have caused the delay), charged that under Hartsfield Atlanta ranked in the top ten cities in murders committed, and accused him of using recorders' court as a source of city revenue by levying fines on persons who should be bound over to a higher court. Under Hartsfield, Brown said, the auditorium stank for lack of air conditioning, though Hartsfield had air-conditioned his own office, and mixed drinks were being openly sold there in violation of the law. Hartsfield responded that Brown was a crybaby who was running around breeding dissension and discord.

Brown did not inject the race issue directly into the debate, as Hartsfield's informant had predicted, so Hartsfield beat him to the punch. Brown, he said, was "going to make the race issue the main plank in his platform for the next campaign. The people of Atlanta will never put up with it."[10] Hartsfield, in fact, seemed to welcome the idea that race would be an issue—and he sat down immediately to draw up a list of accomplishments which would show that he indeed had done all he could to help the Negro, while Brown had not. A few typical items: When the Freedom Train came to Atlanta, the mayor announced to the world that Negro citizens would not be required to go into the train at separate hours, saying he would be proud to view the historic documents with any American citizen. Brown, he said, as county commissioner had required Negro registrants at the courthouse to use separate windows. Hartsfield believed in the Negro police and intended to enlarge their force; there were no Negro police in Fulton County. Hartsfield was building a library for Negro citizens; Fulton County had libraries for its white citizens only.

So politics flared briefly in the spring of 1952 and then went underground, and Hartsfield busied himself with other matters. As usual his interest in Georgia's minerals occupied much of his time and thought, and his correspondence in this field was heavy as he pursued his own personal plan of improvement. One new venture intrigued him. With Jesse Draper and others he went into the vending business in a firm called Koffee Kup, which later was to cause him considerable grief both politically and financially.

Hartsfield in the early fifties could ill afford these ventures. Like many lesser men, he sometimes had problems paying his bills. In March 1952 his grocer, T. L. Lyle, was dunning him for $219.42, and his salary of $13,500, set by the legislature, was hardly enough to support his family, which was more and more beset by sickness. His finance chairman, Aubrey Milam, was planning to push for a raise for him, to $20,000, but with an election coming up in 1953 Hartsfield told him to hold off. He was, however, proud of the fact that the city was in good financial shape. When he went to New York to raise $6 million in bonds for expressways, they sold at a premium.

As vice-president of the American Municipal Association, he spent a long summer traveling throughout the United States, calling on his fellow mayors, meeting with the executive committee of the mayors' group prior to the Democratic Convention in Chicago, where he went to talk about cities and their relationship to the federal government, notably to President Eisenhower, who was cutting back on federal grants to municipalities.

One special trip took him to Shreveport, Louisiana, where on November 8, with his election as president of the mayors' association less than a month away, he was inducted into El Karubah Temple of the Shrine under curiously furtive circumstances. The explanation gives a fascinating insight into the depth, and sometimes the bitterness, of Atlanta politics. Early in November Hartsfield was notified that he should hold himself in readiness for induction into the Shrine by Yaarab Temple in Atlanta. This pleased him, but the date conflicted with the December 3 meeting of the mayors in California, and he asked if he could be inducted into a temple in another city. El Karubah, in Shreveport, agreed to extend this courtesy to Yaarab Temple. Then, on the day he was to be inducted, his political enemies made their move. The following letter from Hartsfield to his good friend Mayor Clyde E. Fant of Shreveport gives some clue to what happened. It was written on November 18, 1952, ten days after the ceremony. "Dear Mayor," wrote Hartsfield:

I hope you will not misunderstand my effort to hide my identity while in Shreveport last November 8.

For your information, Yaarab Temple here has over 6,000 members, a few of whom are highly political, and they have a habit of trying to hold up public officials. I was instructed by the local officials to leave Atlanta incognito and, while in Shreveport, to make no mention of any official connection whatever on account of a small political clique here. It seems that this is standard practice where public officials are involved; consequently, I was carrying out orders when I claimed to be my own cousin.

However, as matters went, it soon became known who I was, and I think several long distance calls were put in and, also, a telegram was sent out there, which procedure did not meet with the approval of the better element of Yaarab Temple here.

I sincerely appreciate the courtesy of your Temple out there in initiating me and I hope next time I see you, I will not be under any orders to remain inconspicuous. Incidentally, I hope you attend the AMA Convention in Los Angeles on December 1.

The next day Mayor Fant replied that he understood perfectly Hartsfield's need to remain incognito while taking the Shrine degree in Shreveport and explained to him what had happened there:

The information that you were here evidently leaked out at Atlanta. We received the wire, with which you are familiar, late in the afternoon. The Potentate called the Divan together to discuss the matter. Since I serve on the Divan, I told the other members that in my opinion, it was entirely political; that such had been used before. A call was placed to Atlanta and your status was cleared by the officers. The Divan accepted my opinion that it was entirely political, but felt that it was best all the way around to have a clearance.

It was a pleasure to have you here, and I shall look forward to seeing you in Los Angeles on December First.

As expected, Hartsfield was elected president of the American Municipal Association on December 1, 1952, making him the mayors' mayor. The convention was in Los Angeles and in Atlanta his associates, in celebrating, cut a huge cake shaped like City Hall. Hartsfield's inaugural speech was a classic example of his foresight concerning the future of American cities. Convinced that transportation was essential to national growth, he urged federal legislation to encourage highway construction.

He plumped for state control of tidelands, and urged a study of liability insurance premiums, which had zoomed in most cities. He stressed the need for cities to find new sources of income other than property taxes, and—with an eye on the election year upcoming—he spoke earnestly of the need to control election expenses in local political campaigns, with the FCC placing stricter controls on a candidate's use of radio and television. He said he would seek a Ford Foundation grant to explore how the problem of flight from the inner city to the suburbs could be controlled, and he offered his fellow mayors a booklet—he had printed five hundred extra—outlining how Atlanta had expanded its boundaries and population under the Plan of Improvement.

The *Constitution* took editorial note of Hartsfield's new honor as president of all the nation's mayors. Hartsfield, the *Constitution* said, "is a remarkable character—a businessman who keeps the city solvent, a politician who seems to relish his enemies, a super-salesman who is never too busy to plug his bailiwick. He is efficient, outspoken, and occasionally witty. It's a safe bet, too, that the nation's mayors will know all there is to know about Atlanta's good points before his term expires."[11] (Hartsfield later told Helen Bullard that the only really influential office in the mayors' association was not the president but the chairman of the resolutions committee.)

YOU'D THINK HE OWNED THE TOWN

HARTSFIELD'S ELECTION to national office as president of the mayors' association, and the prospect that he would be a shoo-in in the 1953 mayor's race in Atlanta, caused Ralph McGill to write his old friend editor Ben Hibbs to suggest Hartsfield as a proper subject for a long piece in the *Saturday Evening Post*. After tracing Hartsfield's accomplishments since 1937 McGill wrote in one revealing and brutally honest paragraph:

He is literally a very difficult man to support, because you get into such a personal rage with him you are almost persuaded to forget he is really a top flight mayor who has done a good job. He always has a tough time because he goes around arguing with people instead of giving them the old political pat on the back.[1]

All this was overcome by the fact that Hartsfield for fifteen years had served a city the size of Atlanta without a hint of corruption. The tentative title the *Post* put on McGill's article, "Mayor of a Showcase City," was accurate enough. But the title that came out in the magazine in October 1953 made the essential point about Hartsfield and his attitude toward the city: "You'd Think He Owns Atlanta." It was a quote from Robert Snodgrass, president of the Atlanta Chamber of Commerce.

By mid-May 1953 Hartsfield did own it, figuratively, for four more years. After a name-calling campaign that had become typical of their contests, he beat Charlie Brown again, by a vote of 32,433 to 25,212. This comfortable victory was due in large part to the political acumen of Helen Bullard. Early in 1953 John Wesley Dobbs had pulled his Republican followers out of the nonpartisan Negro Voters' League, dissatisfied with Hartsfield for his failure to sponsor Negro firemen. Hartsfield's opposition was based on the fact that city firemen shared living quarters; policemen did not.

Bullard went to Grace Hamilton, highly respected Negro leader and a power among her own people in her office as executive director of the Atlanta Urban League, for advice on how this defection might be overcome. The result was a secret memo, undated and unsigned, in which Mrs. Hamilton told Bullard what Hartsfield should say and to whom. She had made up a list of fifty-four black preachers, professors, college presidents, and businessmen—the leaders in the Negro Voters' League—whom Hartsfield should invite to meet with him at the Butler Street YMCA for a talk. Once there, she told Miss Bullard, he should tell them that he recognized there was no single organization that carried sufficient weight with the Negro population to be relied on for complete support. Therefore he was calling upon this group, made up of both Democrats and Republicans, for city politics was a nonpartisan matter. He should begin by saying that his opponents were calling him "the Negroes' representative," but that he denied this. He should say instead that he had tried to be mayor of all the people; that he had been deeply aware of the special needs of the Negro population, but he had had to work on these needs in terms of what was possible for the whole population. He should point out that he had been able to keep city government free of some of the anti-Negro forces so rampant in the state government, but that in this race he strongly believed that his opponent was making a strong effort to turn Atlanta over to those elements in the state, thus punishing him, the mayor, for having resisted them.

It would also be wise, Mrs. Hamilton suggested, to admit

that all had not been done that should have been done—and that the Negro did have legitimate gripes. The sore spots should be brought up and discussed—no Negro firemen, more Negro policemen, better schools and parks for the Negroes, appointment of Negroes to planning boards, and the elimination of police brutality. Bringing all these into the open and discussing them fully would rob the disgruntled of their ammunition. He should then make his plea to the Negro as a citizen, stressing his obligation to register, vote, run for office—all with the motive of what is best for the city, so that all citizens, black and white alike, could benefit. Hartsfield listened, and learned, and won.

Though he came out of the campaign victorious, the usual array of personal problems that had burdened him for years were still with him—the plight of numerous Hartsfield kin in three states, burdened with the cares of old age, illness, financial crises, and an occasional touch of alcoholism, which they looked to "Cousin Willie" to help them solve. He handled each case diplomatically, or brusquely, as he thought best. He was also having problems at home. An anonymous telephone caller had given Pearl, his wife, a report on his alleged romantic attachment to a young secretary. This came as no surprise to her, but it made her even more reluctant to attend his speeches, rallies, and victory celebrations than she had been in the past, for she felt that the whole town knew the story and would be feeling sorry for her. Hartsfield, when she told him of the anonymous call, wrote out a page-long reply to the "contemptible coward" who had made the call, ordering her to read it to the man if he should call again. It is perhaps coincidental that in this year, 1953, Hartsfield went into the hospital for an operation that in the future would spare him the personal and political embarrassment of a possible paternity suit.

As a relief perhaps from family problems, he soon got deeply involved in the projects that charmed him almost as much as did politics—exploration for oil and minerals. With borrowed money he went into a Texas oil-drilling deal. He also began writing to geologist friends around the country, telling them he was ready to hit the woods again in search of minerals, clays, light aggregates—anything he felt would have value when dug out of the Georgia earth. Soon he was deeply involved in something called the Georgia Lightweight Aggregate Company near Rockmart, which produced a product called galite—a trademark patented by Hartsfield—which supposedly made strong lightweight concrete blocks. This, like his other business ventures, failed to catch fire.

In the fall of 1954 he took off again, this time with his fellow mayors, on a tour of the Holy Land, which turned out to be one of the highlights of his career. He came back to write, with great eloquence and deep feeling, an article for the *Journal-Constitution* magazine section on "What I Saw in the Homeland of Jesus." Always quick to put on a costume that might attract photographers, he is pictured in the full regalia of a Bedouin chief, including the burnoose and kaffayeh. The sunwashed streets of the ancient cities, populated with goats and old veiled women selling pots, and old men sitting by crumbling walls, were far different from the bustling streets of Atlanta. He was surprised, though, and highly pleased, to find here some connection with his home city. In Bethlehem, in the Church of the Nativity, the Greek Orthodox archbishop who showed the mayors the spot where Christ reputedly was born, turned out to be a friend of Hartsfield's friend Father Panos Constantinides of Atlanta. He gave Hartsfield a letter to bring home to Father Panos. In Nazareth, where Jesus spent his boyhood, an Arab whose name Hartsfield did not catch told him in broken English that he had a son at Georgia Tech, and the mayor of Nazareth, a Christian Arab, told Hartsfield he was planning to send his son to Tech.

En route to the Holy Land Hartsfield made a midnight tour

of London and noticed that the old city was "much spruced up" since he was there last in 1950. There seemed to be a new spirit in the gray old town, he said. Hartsfield was a great one for assaying the spirit of a city, sensing immediately whether it was one of confidence and progress or apathy and discouragement, and he applied his divining rod to each place he visited. In Athens, where Mayor Constantin Nicolopoulis met them, he made a quick tour of the Parthenon and the Acropolis, made a speech, through an interpreter, complimenting the Greeks on their independence, and went on to Turkey. There he said he found "a real democracy—not afraid of the Russians." The mayor then told him that Turkey had already fought the Russians seventeen times throughout history and would fight them again if need be. Turkey, Hartsfield found, was a land of free enterprise, and many American manufacturers were moving there to build factories and warehouses. In one respect he found Turkish enterprise was too free. A city official offered him a glass of some brown liquid purported to be Coca-Cola. Hartsfield took a healthy gulp, gagged, sputtered, and spat it out.

The Turks, for all their enterprise, were backward in many ways. An American agricultural mission found that the Turks were burning cottonseed to get rid of it and feeding their cows on hay. The Americans, Hartsfield reported, taught them to mix hay with cottonseed meal; the cows fattened quickly, gave much more milk, and were healthier.

In Beirut, at the Saint George Hotel, Hartsfield was delighted to run into two friends from Atlanta, Mr. and Mrs. Carlyle Fraser. They visited the American University, financed mainly by Americans, where three thousand students from fifty-one countries were enrolled. This, said Hartsfield, was one of the finest contributions we could make to the better understanding of Americans in the Middle East.

In Damascus, whose history goes back six thousand years, Hartsfield walked down The Street Called Straight, to try to find the house where Ananias—the man who was told in a vision to restore Paul's sight—had lived. A modern house had been built on the spot, and the ruins could no longer be seen—a disappointment to Hartsfield, who at home sought to preserve all ancient landmarks.

A mayor's duties were much the same anywhere in the world, Hartsfield found. They must answer the complaints of citizens, but he felt that the mayor of Damascus had things pretty easy. His main problem at the moment, he told Hartsfield, had to do with roosters crowing so loudly they woke the neighbors. (Hartsfield, deadpan, asked him if the cocks crowed thrice, or just once.)

En route to Jordan, Hartsfield's party passed a number of refugee camps. In Jordan there was an air of tension, soldiers were everywhere, and he had the feeling that Jordan's King Hussein believed that his country had been betrayed by the Truman administration's support of Israel. In the Arab quarter of Jerusalem the mayor, an Arab, took Hartsfield and his friends on a tour of the holy places, the Garden of Gethsemane, the Mosque of Omar, supposedly set on the foundation of Solomon's Temple, and the Church of the Holy Sepulchre. From the balcony of his hotel room he could see the Mount of Olives.

Passing through the Mandelbaum Gate into Israeli Jerusalem, he found the atmosphere completely different. Crossing the border, from Jordan into Israel, he wrote, was like stepping out of ancient time into the lobby of a modern American hotel. The clothing was European, the language, English or Hebrew. And everywhere people were at work. "Jews were digging ditches, running air compressors, driving trucks, doing all the hard work necessary in any frontier country."[2] In Tel Aviv new buildings were under construction. In Haifa the mayor, who had visited Hartsfield in Atlanta not long before, returned the favor by walking Hartsfield to exhaustion, showing off the wonders of his town.

Israel, said Hartsfield, was moving strongly toward an economy in which industry, agriculture, shipping, and transportation would be in balance. Her success would depend, he said,
on the Middle East remaining at peace—and that was doubtful.
The whole Middle East, he said, was potentially explosive, particularly in the Arab countries where the little man was waking
up to the fact that he had always been given a raw deal. He did
not believe, however, that the Arab countries would turn to
communism, for the religion of Allah was too strong.

He came back with the conviction that the United Nations
was much more than a debating society with offices in New
York. In the Arab countries they were doing much to help. So,
he said, was the United States, though in a different way, as
American business began moving, tentatively, into that area.

From Tel Aviv the mayor's party flew on to Rome, where
they had a long conference with Ambassador Clare Booth Luce
and an audience with Pope Pius XII. Best remembered by the
mayors, though, was Hartsfield's visit to the Sistine Chapel.
There, after walking about like the others, peering up at the
ceiling paintings by Michelangelo, he pulled out a bench that
probably had not been moved for eons, lay down upon it, and
studied the famous frescoes in comfort. To a startled guard he
explained that cots should be provided so that visitors would
not get a crick in their necks.

Atlanta went into 1954 with the same old mayor, but he was
working with a new form of city government. In January the
old bicameral system of city council and board of aldermen
was replaced with a single body—a board of aldermen made up
of two members from each ward, which it was hoped would be
a more responsive and efficient form of government. The city,
as in all the years of Hartsfield's administration, ended the year
free of debt, though it had spent well over a million dollars on
general improvements, including sewer extension, new streets
and bridges, and the addition of a swimming pool to Candler

Park. Nearly three million dollars had been spent in expanding the water system, and the old city auditorium at last was air-conditioned, presumably silencing Hartsfield's critics who had complained that it was redolent of perspiring wrestlers, basketball players, and operatic tenors. (Hartsfield, who once carried a spear in one of the early operas, loved to tell the story of the time he was accepting a bust of Caruso as a gift to the city, to be placed in the auditorium. A slightly befuddled wrestling fan who was standing by was confused when the bust was unveiled. "Hey, Bill, who was this Buster Caruso you been talking about? He don't look like no rassler to me.")

Though the first four years of the decade had seen much progress, there were ominous financial clouds hanging over the city in 1954. The city's cash carry-over, usually somewhere around two million dollars, was down by nearly half a million dollars, a danger signal, according to Hartsfield. There were several reasons for this. Business conditions, after a modest boom set off by the Korean War, had leveled off and tax collections were down by 5 percent. To carry out the Plan of Improvement meant that 155 new employees had been hired, adding about $410,000 to the city's payrolls. Automatic salary raises would add about $215,000 more to the amount. All this meant that new sources of revenue had to be found, not by cutting back on its services, but by finding new sources of income.

"The basic condition of our city is thoroughly sound," he told the aldermanic board:

We are still on a cash basis and hope to remain there. But if we are to continue good service and do the many things which our citizens demand, we must have more revenues . . . Our increases in the cost of government have been very moderate, in the face of enormous new collections by other governments around us . . . I recommend that during the year 1954 a long range study be made of Atlanta's revenue problems; . . . and I call upon our citizens, our newspapers and our business leaders to give their aid and support. If Atlanta is to be gradually pushed to the wall, while other governments all around us are lush with revenue, then the final result is not hard to predict. Insufficient revenues breed civic dissatisfaction, poor service and general complaints. This in turn runs good men out of government and turns it over to bad officials who care nothing for their reputations as long as they can get control of the public till and its collateral perquisites.[3]

It was Hartsfield's habit, even in palmiest times, to picture Atlanta as surrounded by jealous and predatory governments determined to do it harm; and though he thanked the legislature for their aid in pushing through the expressways in the past, he urged that they move with even greater alacrity in the future. The city, he pointed out, could not buy rights-of-way until detailed route maps had been prepared, and the state highway department had been slow in doing this. (Hartsfield, for all his progressive views, was always stubbornly wrong in one of his ideas regarding highway construction. He felt that no expressway would ever need more than three lanes in each direction. Atlanta traffic soon refuted this, and the city in after years had to spend millions buying extra rights-of-way and widening bridges.)

As the year wore on, one of Hartsfield's old interests, the Empire Oil Company of Texas, dissolved; but Hartsfield, ever hopeful that someday oil or minerals would make him rich, dug up $516.60 to buy shares in a new company formed out of the wreckage of the old, its main assets a drilling rig and two diesel trucks. Any suggestion of mineral wealth anywhere excited Hartsfield, and at the same time, during 1954, he was writing his friends the geologists asking their judgment of a new method of searching for oil by what seemed to be surface methods of reaching underlying strata. At the same time he was writing a Venezuelan geologist, asking him about the prospect of finding minerals there "which can be mined through moderate investments, and not oil or iron ore or any other resources which required millions in corporate funds." If there were such prospects, he said, he would like to come to Caracas and bring a geologist friend with him. Along with his interest in mining, his old showman's instincts were hard at work; he was offering to help his son-in-law, James Cheshire, set up children's amusement parks, complete with miniature trains, merry-go-rounds, and other attractions on the roofs of department stores in Atlanta. Nothing came of it.

An event late in 1954 brought Hartsfield both sorrow and a sense of relief. Miss Claudia Hartsfield, "Cousin Claude," whose health and financial condition had been of great concern to all the Hartsfield clan for years, died at the age of eighty-nine. A former Atlanta schoolteacher, she had once taught "Willie," and her letter of congratulations, scrawled in pencil on lined paper, was always among the first he read after he won an election.

McGill's story about Hartsfield in the *Saturday Evening Post* brought letters from Hartsfields all over the country, many of them claiming kin, all of them asking for genealogical information, and most of them speaking of him in laudatory terms as the most famous bearer of the Hartsfield name. Hartsfield was never one to disparage his own achievements, and when the Atlanta Civic, Social, and Cultural Register selected him as one of the outstanding representatives of the city, who had made a major contribution to Atlanta's social, cultural, and civic development, he was highly pleased to be so glowingly described. When the Lewis Historical Publishing Company, the original publisher of Franklin Garrett's *Atlanta and Environs,* asked him for a brief biography, his own appraisal of what he had achieved in his years as alderman, legislator, and mayor, was factual enough and accurately summed up his public contribution.

Some of his outstanding achievements have been his advocacy of expanding aviation facilities, the development of the Chattahoochee River, the installation of a model budget law, under which Atlanta has operated upon a cash basis for fifteen years, the beautification of downtown Atlanta through the building of Hurt and Plaza Parks, and the Expressway system. Also, during the administration of Mayor Hartsfield, Atlanta adopted the famous "Plan of Improvement," under which certain functions of the City and Fulton County were re-grouped, together with a large-scale enlargement of Atlanta's city limits from 37 to 128 square miles, with consequent large increase in population.[4]

His taste for travel was indulged again as the year drew to a close. In November he was again in Germany, as a guest of the West German government, and had a thirty-minute talk with Chancellor Adenauer.

As he began 1955 Hartsfield could look back on the year just past with a certain satisfaction. The new form of government with a mayor and a board of aldermen had worked fairly well. The school board, with its first black member, Dr. Rufus Clement, providing the leadership, was to receive half of a ten-million-dollar-bond issue as it began to prepare for the inevitable day when Atlanta schools would be integrated. The rest went for fifty-nine miles of new sewers and street improvements. The northeast expressway was completed to Piedmont Avenue, and $200,000 was spent in expressway lights. Near Hartsfield's old birthplace on Butler Street, a new Grady Hospital was under construction, new tennis centers were started, and the Piedmont Park Art Festival—Art in the Park—began. To Hartsfield it was a happy mixture of a city's services to its people, touching as it did on health, transport, education, sports, garbage disposal, and the arts.

In process of completion was a $150,000 project for clearing the approaches to the airport runway, giving Hartsfield a chance to give the back of his hand to other aviation centers. "Monstrosity passenger terminals built by misguided civic braggarts in other towns do not make an airport," he said. On the other hand, "our great airport, one of the most important in the nation, now has runways, high intensity lights, naviga-

tional aids, and approaches which enable the mightiest congregation of civic airplanes anywhere in the world to arrive and
depart there within an hour's time."[5]

This was Hartsfield's answer to the "jealous and disgruntled
people" who held that the recent improvements to the airport's
ground facilities, of which Hartsfield was so proud, were not
enough. A new terminal, he pointed out, and the needed parking ramps, passenger terminals, taxi strips, parking areas, and
additional access roads would cost nearly eight million dollars.
All these would come in time, but they would require a bond
issue and federal help, which had temporarily been discon-
tinued. The city had ended the year with a cash carry-over of
more than two million dollars, and in view of this he thought
nearly everybody in city government should have a raise.

He ended on his usual note of pride and hope. "And so—my
friends and fellow workers, our city enters into the new year in
good financial condition and with sound and intelligent plans
for future expansion. True, we do not have the millions to do
everything that would be desirable. And again we must appeal
to the state for additional sources of revenue if we are to en-
gage in a huge bond issue for future expressways and other
needs of a big city. But somehow, Atlanta always meets the
challenge . . . We have been doing it, and will continue in the
years to come."[6]

Hartsfield celebrated his sixty-fifth birthday in 1955 but kept
on traveling abroad and working at home with the zest of a
young man. His mind was teeming with possible money-raising
projects. Spring found him joining with friends in financing the
Downtown Motel and traveling to Venezuela to talk with
United States Steel geologists about the possibility of finding
nonferrous metals there.

Among city projects the airport was never far from his
thoughts, and he made several trips to Washington, pressing
the Eisenhower administration to reverse its policy of cutting

back on federal aid to airports. In this endeavor he spoke not only as the mayor of Atlanta, but as chairman of the American Municipal Association's airport committee, speaking for all the mayors. While in Washington on airport matters, he would also push hard with other agencies for support of another of his favorite projects—Buford Dam. Hartsfield had been at the groundbreaking in 1950, and now the Corps of Engineers was at work at the dam site, bulldozing the lake bed, but eleven million dollars more was needed if the dam was to be finished by the target date of 1956. His arguments were potent in both cases. To him the airport and the dam were equally important to the future of the city. The dam would impound the Chatta-hoochee north of Atlanta, forming a lake that would insure Atlanta an adequate water supply for generations to come. It would benefit not only Atlanta but all the area, as a flood con-trol, hydroelectric, and recreation area development. As for the airport, Atlanta had already outgrown it. Its landing facilities could handle the biggest planes and control heavy traffic at peak periods, but the loading zones and the passenger facilities were already inadequate, even after expansion a few years earlier.

The federal agencies moved too slowly to suit Hartsfield, so in May 1955 he announced bluntly that, federal help or no federal help, the city would go ahead with an eight-million-dollar program of airport improvement, to be financed by revenue certificates. He did not let up in his pressure on Wash-ington though, urging that the federal government set aside at least a hundred million in the 1956 budget, to be matched by the cities. His argument was simple: there was no point in building bigger, faster aircraft if there were few airports in the United States that could handle them.

Finally Washington listened. President Eisenhower in Sep-tember signed the bill providing $252 million in federal funds for airport construction, of which Atlanta's share would be some three million dollars. In tribute to Hartsfield's efforts, his Republican friend Robert Snodgrass sent him the pen with which Ike had signed the airport bill.

While battling for the airport and for Buford Dam, Hartsfield had time to make a quick trip to France and Germany under the auspices of the Crusade for Freedom. Near Berchtesgaden he was photographed launching a gas-filled balloon to carry propaganda leaflets over Iron Curtain countries. He also made a side trip to Belgium to visit his former Atlanta friends Mildred and Paul Seydell. He came home to tell all his friends that what he had predicted two years earlier had come true. *Gone With the Wind* had proved to be a great hit in Free Europe and was still playing in Paris and Berlin after two years.

Talking to the Hungry Club in March, Hartsfield spoke at length of the blueprints Atlanta had made to improve the lot of its Negro citizens, citing slum clearance and the greatly improved streets, sidewalks, and lighting facilities in the black communities. Before the year was out he had the chance to back up his words with action. After a bitter fight in which many citizens urged that the city golf courses be closed, Hartsfield shortly before Christmas ordered that they be opened to Negro golfers. His only explanation: it was the right thing to do. All the facilities of the city, including parks and golf courses, belonged to its citizens, and Atlanta's Negroes were its citizens, growing daily more important to its progress. It was as simple as that.

Hartsfield possibly received less criticism for his desegregation of the golf course than he did for one of his personal money-making projects. Early in 1955, using money borrowed from the Trust Company and the C&S Bank, he bought a tenth interest in a business called Koffee Kup, which at the time, he said later, was operating a vending business outside Atlanta. Among its shareholders were former Governor Herman Talmadge and Hartsfield's friend Alderman Jesse Draper. Shortly after changing from a partnership to a corporation in 1954, Koffee Kup started moving into Atlanta, replacing competing vendors at the airport parking lot, the telephone company, a new building at Georgia State University, and various other places around town. To have the mayor connected with any firm that might depend even partially on political influence for its prosperity was obviously against the public interest, and as soon as Hartsfield's connection became known a great outcry arose, led by his political critics, George Biggers in particular. It was the first time even the faintest breath of financial scandal had touched the Hartsfield administration; the town was shocked and made its disappointment known.

Hartsfield resigned from the corporation "within sixty seconds" after he found out that they were doing business in Atlanta.[7] He sold his shares to Bobby Dodd, Georgia Tech coach, and in time the tempest in the Koffee Kup blew over. For Hartsfield the whole enterprise had been a financial and political loss. He was never discouraged, though, in keeping a sharp eye out for honest ways in which he or his friends might improve either their political image or their financial lot. When the Ringling Brothers and Barnum and Bailey Circus came to town late in 1955, he learned that the famous old show was having financial difficulties. To Hartsfield, a circus buff, it seemed that the greatest show on earth could well become an adjunct of what he firmly believed to be the greatest drink on earth—Coca-Cola. When circus management seemed interested, he went to his friend Robert Woodruff with the idea. A personal letter from Hartsfield to a circus official tells what happened:

About the matter we discussed while you were here, involving a certain soft drink company. I mentioned this matter to the top man, and they were not interested.

Had you ever thought of turning this institution into a stock company, and letting the public in?

Please don't think me meddlesome. I am just a great believer in the circus tradition and want to see it go on in the future, regardless of death or taxes.[8]

For Hartsfield the year was a difficult one financially. His salary of $16,000 was not only drained by unfortunate business ventures but by heavy doctors' bills. Pearl Hartsfield was ill throughout much of the year and so was Fannie Lee Bettis, the highly efficient secretary in Hartsfield's Grant Building office, from which he conducted all his nonpolitical activities. Devoted to him, and sharing his interests both in politics and business, Miss Bettis had sold her war bonds to provide money to finance some of his mineral ventures, and in times of political crisis she had manned the telephone to pass the word of Hartsfield's wishes. Never one to forget a loyal friend, Hartsfield assumed the responsibility for her doctors' bills, which in her last years amounted to several thousand dollars. Also, in the event that he should die before she did, he named her in his will, giving her a two-fifths interest in one of his insurance policies—the other three-fifths going to his wife.

Though Hartsfield himself went into 1956 pretty well strapped for cash, the city, for the eighteenth consecutive year of his administration, was in excellent shape. All its bills had been paid promptly, saving more than $27,000 in cash discounts, and there was a cash carry-over of $2.5 million, the biggest in the city's history. For all the wizardry with which he managed the city's funds, though, Hartsfield frequently got his own finances in a mess. Once, in his early days as mayor, his daughter, Mildred, very much needed a warm coat to wear to school. Hartsfield was broke and it was Mrs. Hartsfield who solved the problem. She sold the little diamond Hartsfield had given her as an engagement ring and used the money to buy the coat. Like many of his fellow Atlantans, he often had to borrow on his insurance, was sometimes late in filing his federal income tax returns, and in 1956 caused himself considerable embarrassment by failing to pay his local taxes on time. A fi fa was issued against city taxes of $156.34 and county taxes of $62.53 on his residence at 637 Pelham Road. He could possibly derive some comfort from the fact that about 5 percent of city and county taxpayers were also delinquent, among them the chairman of the county commission, James H. Aldredge. On the other hand, he would sometimes forget that he had paid a local bill and would send a second check, confusing his creditors.

In this year also he had to turn down an opportunity to invest $1,500 for a one-third interest in an oil well venture in Texas. "Sorry," he wrote to the promoter, who had drilled several dry holes for him before. "I have no money to invest."[9] Fortunately for Hartsfield the legislature in 1956 raised the mayor's salary from $16,000 to $20,000 a year.

Hartsfield's straitened financial circumstances, which required him to sell at a very slim profit his interest in the Lightweight Aggregate Company and to get out of the Downtown Motel organization, did nothing to lessen the esteem in which he was held by his more well-to-do friends. In March he was writing to John O. Chiles, who over the years was his chief political fund raiser, Dick Garlington, and Robert MacDougald, who was a partner in his mineral interests, telling them: "There are no words with which to tell you how much I appreciated the thoughtfulness and friendship that prompted you to get up that beautiful birthday party for me." To Robert Woodruff, another sponsor of the bash at the Capital City Club, he sent a telegram of thanks. He was sixty-six and was feeling fairly frisky, for he had just had an excellent report from Mason Lowance, his doctor. There was evidence of an old ulcer, now well healed, and there was a slightly irregular heartbeat, which had been showing up in his cardiogram for the past five or six years, but these were nothing to worry about. The doctor ended his report with

the hope that the mayor would have an excellent year and that
he could have "a little decrease in business stress as the years
go by."[10]

The year was indeed one of the less stressful ones that Hartsfield had known. He went to the opera; he put air conditioning
in the house on Pelham Road, to the great delight of Mrs.
Hartsfield who now only rarely left the house. He took time out
from his duties to give the Macon Boy Scout troop to which his
grandson, Monty Cheshire, belonged a guided tour of the museum in the state capitol, the zoo, and the Cyclorama. He wrote
a long letter to a nephew, Charles Hartsfield, a soldier stationed
at Heidelberg, sending him twenty-five dollars and telling him
to use it to go to Paris; no man's life was complete, he said, if
he had not seen Paris. Though he was a dedicated Adlai Stev-
enson man, and turned over his office to him for conferences
while in Atlanta, he welcomed Richard Nixon to a rally given
by Atlanta's Young Republicans in Hurt Park. He went out to
Fort Bliss, Texas, by invitation of the military, to observe the
guided-missile center there, and he was pleased to be inducted
into the Ancient and Honorable Order of the Oozlefinch, with
the degree of "24-hour Expert." This entitled him to "fly tail
foremost and to wear ear plugs and blinders at all occasions attended by the weaker sex."[11] He went with aldermen Jesse
Draper and Ralph Huie to California for a tour of Disneyland.
His final foray of the year was into Mexico for the opening of
the Continental Hilton in Mexico City. There with Mayor de-
Lesseps Morrison of New Orleans and Governor Allen Shivers
of Texas, he attended bullfights, cocktail parties, and gala
black-tie dinners. To him, though, the most impressive part of
the dedication was not social but religious, when the archbishop
of Mexico, in full regalia, blessed the hotel in solemn ritual. On
a side trip to Acapulco for a beach luncheon he was pleased to
run into many old New York and Hollywood friends.

For all his obsession with Atlanta and its affairs, Hartsfield was always eager to know what was going on in the rest of the world. A man fanatically addicted to the media, in his house on Pelham Road he had something to listen to in every room—eight radios, three television sets, a combination radio-phonograph, a high-fidelity record player, a wire recorder, and a tape recorder. Traveling to his office in his car he listened to police calls on a shortwave radio, or news on the regular car radio. At the office he could listen to what was going on in council chambers while he worked at his desk. His first act on getting up in the morning was to tune in on the news. At night his routine was similar. Wherever he was, a radio was always somewhere near at hand. Finally getting home, late at night, he would turn on a shortwave police radio on one side of the bed and a powerful shortwave on the other side with which he could range the world, picking up foreign stations. One of his favorites was Moscow. "This way," he told an interviewer, "I can keep up all the time with what's going on in Atlanta and all the world. I tell people I'm an electronic mayor. Actually, I'm just a gadget bug."[12]

When Hartsfield gave his 1956 report to the aldermen, he obviously had in mind that 1957 was to be an election year. Again the city was in sound financial shape with well over a million dollars in cash on hand after all debts had been paid. This had been accomplished, Hartsfield pointed out proudly, while the city provided the expanded services it had guaranteed its new citizens under the Plan of Improvement, which had just completed its fifth year. There were now 503,000 people inside the city limits and 885,000 in all in the metropolitan area. To serve this huge constituency the city had spent more than nine million dollars in the past five years on water service alone, laying 435 miles of pipe and installing more than 25,000 meters and nearly 4,000 hydrants.

Within four years, he predicted, there would be a million people in the metro area—which meant that the citizens would have to authorize millions more in additional funds to keep pace with the population growth. In the course of this litany of water lines and sewers laid and streets paved and tons of garbage disposed of, Hartsfield made one prophetic forecast. The huge open space over the railroad tracks adjacent to Spring Street would in time be covered over, he said, from the viaduct level. And upon it would be built a fabulous real-estate development. He did not predict its form or shape, but here was outlined the idea of the Omni—the vast sports, commercial, and hotel center that now rises over the railroad right-of-way.

Rarely did Hartsfield and the black leaders get their signals crossed, but it did happen briefly in 1957. The fact that Atlanta blacks still had to sit in the back of the bus was galling, and the bus boycott in Montgomery by Martin Luther King, Jr., in 1955 and 1956 had brought it to the forefront of Negro grievances. In January 1957, without first consulting Hartsfield or notifying Chief Jenkins, whose police would have to defend them against outraged segregationists, a group of black ministers boarded a bus in downtown Atlanta and took their seats in the white section. The driver wanted no part of such lawlessness. He drove the bus, still carrying the ministers, back to the garage. There they quietly got off and went home.

Hartsfield was livid at having been taken by surprise. He got Chief Jenkins on the phone in a shouting rage. As always, though, even in a temper tantrum his mind was clicking coolly toward a solution. At his direction Jenkins would set up a situation whereby the law that required separate seating could be tested in the courts. He told Jenkins to get the black leaders on the phone and arrange for their arrest. Jenkins called Dr. William Holmes Borders, leader of the ministers, and outlined his plan. He would send out the Black Maria to an agreed-upon spot. The ministers would arrive, seek to board a bus, and be arrested. They would then be taken down to jail and booked, with photographers and reporters present to be sure the arrest was widely publicized. The Black Maria was actually Dr. Borders's idea from the start, thwarted when the driver went back to the garage instead of calling the police. Borders thought it would give their cause national recognition if the town's oldest and most dignified black preachers were shown being hauled away in the paddy wagon. It was hoped that this would cause the state to back off from its plan to enforce segregated seating if the city failed to do so. Then a test case could be heard in federal court, where segregated seating laws would almost certainly be thrown out. The courts in due course did declare segregated seating unlawful, and Hartsfield, with Jenkins's help, again had saved his city from embarrassment. There was no boycott, no interruption of transportation, no protest beyond a few glares and mutterings, when blacks began to sit wherever they pleased.

Hartsfield, as he laid his plans for reelection, had much going for him. The airport was one of his greatest talking points. It was, he proudly pointed out, the fifth busiest in the nation and one of the busiest in the world. It employed fifty-five hundred people at an annual payroll of over twenty-five million dollars. It produced 10 percent more business than the Paris airport, and twice as much as the Rome. It put six hundred thousand dollars a year into the city's coffers from landing fees and concession rentals. At Hartsfield's urging the city was in the mood to make it even bigger, even busier. Two million dollars in revenue certificates had already been issued to start a program for financing a modern terminal that would cost at least fifteen million dollars. In case there were frugal souls who deplored such expenditures, Hartsfield pointed out that all this would come back in a few years in increased fees for airline and concessions. Actually, he argued, Atlanta was being conservative. Dallas was planning to spend sixteen million dollars in local funds; Los Angeles, fifty-four million; San Francisco, thirty-five million.

Airport expenditures were only a pittance compared to the other sums Atlanta needed to spend. For these Hartsfield pushed for the biggest bond issue in Atlanta's history—nearly fifty-two million dollars, for schools, sewers, traffic improvement, the airport terminal, and expanded water systems. Atlanta's water supply was now assured for generations to come. North of Atlanta, Buford Dam, which had been Hartsfield's baby from the start, was beginning to impound the muddy surging waters of the Chattahoochee River. Among those who wished to pay tribute to Hartsfield for the part he had played in this vast project was an organization calling itself the Upper Chattahoochee Development Association, made up of businessmen from communities along the Chattahoochee from DeKalb and Fulton north into the mountain counties. On the night of March 1, 1957 they gave a huge party for Hartsfield at the Dixie Ballroom of the Henry Grady Hotel, honoring him on his birthday for the work he had done in promoting the dam and the huge thirty-seven-thousand-acre Lake Lanier which was beginning to rise behind it. The date also marked the seventh anniversary of the groundbreaking for the dam, which had occurred on this same date in 1950, with Hartsfield much in evidence.

The building of the dam and lake was all well enough for insuring Atlanta's water supply, providing recreation for its citizens, and creating hydroelectric power, but it was only a small part of the plans that Hartsfield had for the Chattahoochee. To him the river was Atlanta's most priceless and indispensable asset, and in the years after the dam was built, he still pushed hard for down-river development that would make the Chattahoochee navigable from Columbus to Atlanta. Despite the pressure he brought to bear on the Corps of Engineers, the Rivers and Harbors Commission, on congressmen, senators, civic clubs, and anybody else who would listen, this huge project never came off, and he was denied the joy of seeing steamboats at the landing in Atlanta.

The birthday party for Hartsfield packed most of Atlanta's leaders in business and finance, as well as politics, into the Dixie Ballroom. C. B. Culpepper, chairman of the Atlanta Freight Bureau, delivered the salute to Hartsfield. He did not wish to present Hartsfield as either a saint, a genius, or an expert, he said. He was, though, "a man who knows what to do, and gets it done," "a man of courage and fidelity," "a good mayor who had kept his city in sound financial condition," on a high progressive plane, and "so completely free from graft and corruption as to make it the envy of the entire nation."[13]

Hartsfield's political instincts told him that it would be a good time to announce his candidacy for mayor while this glowing tribute was still ringing in the public ear. As a result, a week later, on March 7 he announced that he once again would run. His ten-year-old grandson Monty Cheshire, son of the mayor's daughter Mildred, came up from Macon to stand with his grandfather, proudly passing his $2,500 qualification fee to Sam Massell, secretary of the City Executive Committee.

Two problems, Hartsfield realized, would confront him as he entered this race. Somehow he must manage to keep peace between black and white in a campaign that would have to recognize a growing pressure from the blacks for equal opportunity in all fields. Second, he must be able to convey to Atlantans, particularly his friends in the "establishment," his own great dream of Atlanta's future.

Though Hartsfield wrote his own speeches, and woe be to the typist who changed a comma or an exclamation point, he leaned heavily on Helen Bullard, political analyst George Goodwin, and others of his advisors for ideas. An undated unsigned rough draft of a speech to a business group was a source of much help to him. It began with the statement that Atlanta was in the midst of tremendous change and that the business community had more at stake and would have more to do with shaping politics for this new era than any other individuals. Up to now he and they had worked together for the good of corporate Atlanta as it moved toward a population of half a million. But during the fifty years when this was going on, the whole pattern of urban life in America—and especially in Atlanta—had changed. The problems ahead were not those of a corporate city of half a million but those of a closely knit, expanding regional area of a million people. All this had happened much more quickly than had been expected. At first it was predicted that there would be a million people in the metro area by 1980. It now was clear that this population would be reached by 1960 or 1961—an unforeseen result of the speed and magnitude of the South's change from an agricultural to an industrial economy. In the next few years Atlanta would be scattered over six or more counties. The city was now the heart of a vast highway network, with six of the great new interstate highways meeting there—an event that had not been expected before 1990. Now the people of Griffin were closer to Atlanta, in travel time, than the people of Roswell or Lithonia.

All this meant new responsibility for Atlanta's public officials and businessmen, who could no longer be concerned only with corporate Atlanta. They would have to work with, and help, six or eight counties and three times as many municipalities, just to meet the problems of Atlanta's own expansion. The big problems—traffic, metropolitan plans, health, police—were regional, not city-wide alone.

Drastic new ways of moving goods and people throughout the Atlanta region would have to be worked out. Expressways were only one answer; rail and rapid transit must also be developed. Areas in the city left dead or dying as population moved outward must be renewed; industrial districts of various sizes and functions must be planned, built, and serviced. And to serve these renewed areas and outlying municipalities, corporate Atlanta's services would have to branch out through the region, providing city water, sewer service, fire and police protection, and offering parks, airports, and library facilities to its neighbors under contract. These expanded services meant that city administration might have to be expanded (the mayor's office force had not been increased in twenty years). It all added up to the fact that the leaders of the region, in the city and out, would have to start thinking about a regional government, about new city-county relationships that could provide efficient municipal services all over the region, with all the people having adequate representation.

These were essentially the type of problems that businessmen were used to solving—the problems facing a big national corporation with a lot of subdivisions. For Atlanta to continue its fantastic progress, the city would need all the management techniques that business had perfected. The regional city in the automobile age, the draft pointed out, is something entirely new. To meet its challenge the mayor would have to have the help of businessmen. The challenge was far bigger than any the city had ever faced before. But it could be met, the memo said, "by planning where we are going and going there together."

Such was the calm and rational Hartsfield pitch to the members of the business community, and they listened and applauded. In facing audiences less sympathetic to his cause his approach was entirely different. Suave, poised, humorous, urbane, and witty when presiding over a library opening or welcoming the Metropolitan Opera to Atlanta, before an unfriendly audience he was a rough-tongued brawler on the platform, and he used words that cut and bruised like knives and hammers.

His opponent, Archie Lindsay, soon identified Hartsfield as the "NAACP candidate," and a growing Ku Klux Klan influence in the community used even harsher language. Once, at a speech in southwest Atlanta, he came into a house already aroused to fury against him by earlier speakers. As he came down the aisle the angry crowd denounced him. "Go home, nigger lover, go home, nigger lover," they chanted. Face set, he went on to the rostrum and stood there glaring stonily down at the standing mob. Suddenly, he thrust his hands above his head, looking momentarily ten feet tall. "Shut up!" he bellowed. Shocked and startled, the crowd fell silent. Then, his voice hard and grating, he spoke, every word strong and clear.

"I didn't ask to come out here . . . You asked me to come. Now, are you going to listen to me? . . . Or are you going to keep on acting like a bunch of bums?" "What do you want me to do," he went on, "put on a bed sheet and go out and burn a few crosses? . . . You want me to go out and dynamite a few houses? Tell me . . . what do you want me to do?"

Nobody answered, and he went on telling Atlanta's story. While they were going around peddling hate and discord, he said, Atlanta was moving ahead. He then went into his campaign pitch—of Atlanta's past progress and its future challenge. When he finally finished, he walked out to wild applause.[14]

Hartsfield won the May primary, earning a sixth consecutive term with 37,612 votes to Archie Lindsay's 33,808. The mayor, only half in jest, attributed his victory to the support of his ten-year-old grandson. Monty had appeared with his grandfather on television late in the campaign, and at the end of the mayor's speech, he looked straight at the camera and said slowly and very clearly, and without coaching, "I hope you will vote for my grandfather, for I think he is a good man." Hartsfield's response: "Monty, that was the best political speech I ever heard."[15] Monty, it seems, also had some of his grandfather's sense of humor. One Christmas he sent Hartsfield a card signed "Your strongest supporter." It carried a picture of a ladies' girdle.

Early in the campaign an issue arose that caused Hartsfield deep concern: a grand jury investigation showed that the "bug," the workers' lottery, was thriving in Atlanta, the implication being that Chief Herbert Jenkins's police department might bear looking into, since no lottery could thrive if the police were on their toes. Archie Lindsay made much of this, and Hartsfield decided to hit the issue head on. Certainly, he said, when elected he would immediately call for a full and complete investigation of the police. If there was any crookedness there those responsible would be fired forthwith. One outgrowth of the investigation was the formation of a metropolitan vice squad.

The race physically debilitated Hartsfield, though he had been consuming in considerable quantities specially prepared vitamins and minerals which he ordered from a supplier in California. A reporter remembers him, for the first time, becoming exhausted as he walked about his office, shouting his denunciation of his political opponents. He sat down on a reclining chair, pushed it all the way back, and lay flat upon it, continuing to shout and wave his arms. Though he anticipated no trouble in winning the general election in December, he lost no time in getting his advisors together to lay plans for the future. Both papers had supported Hartsfield in the primary, but he felt the warmth of their endorsement was not as fervent as it might be. So plans were laid for personally cultivating the higher executives over a period of time, in the hope that he could win their lasting friendship and support. With the mayor's penchant for riling the high brass, it was suggested that for the present it might be more effective if a third party took over the job of wooing. When a more cordial atmosphere was created, the direct approach could be resumed. The immediate need was for the mayor to reestablish himself as the true leader in Atlanta. He must not be a follower of the papers or of grand juries; he must lead. The grand jury and the papers had scolded him fairly roughly about the way his police were failing to handle the lottery operators, but he must rise above such criticism, his advisors told him. He must become a fountainhead of good and sound, but exciting, ideas for taking Atlanta into her second million citizens. He must put these ideas before the public as the program for "New Atlanta"—which would be the slogan for the next burst of progress. One of the highlights of this program must be urban renewal, with some civic authority such as Phil Hammer talking about better ways for people to live, stamping out the breeding places of crime and discontent, the importance of urban renewal, not only to downtown Atlanta but the entire metropolitan area. Hartsfield must push hard for this program, as he had pushed for annexation.

As mayor of all the people, he must stress the importance of the Negro citizen, building up pride among white citizens about the way Atlanta was solving the problem of separate races living together in the same big thriving community. Negro purchasing power must be emphasized, and blacks must be put on citizens' committees, since this was simply the fair Atlanta way of doing things. (Hartsfield in the past had strongly opposed a biracial committee, for its deliberations would be in public view. He preferred to work quietly, behind the scenes.)

Mass transportation must be stressed. The presidents of the railroads serving Atlanta should be called in and urged to produce plans immediately for a railborne rapid-transit system. Hint at subsidy, tell them the city will help with money, planning, and other details, the memo suggested.

Talk about water, and how Atlanta stands ready to provide water, residential and industrial, to the entire metropolitan area.

Discussion of parks and recreation areas should stress exciting separate areas. Fernbank should be acquired by the city, and a children's zoo should be developed, there or in Piedmont Park, featuring domesticated and native animals, and snakes, and a cage large enough for birds to fly in. A real Confederate memorial museum should be developed in connection with the

Cyclorama. A civic theater should be built, a civic center, a new little park should be created, perhaps at Peachtree and West Peachtree, and Decatur Street should be completely re-built from Five Points to the expressway.

These exciting programs should be hatched off one after an-other, giving the citizens something to think about—and ap-prove—every day until the election in December. The mayor and the board of aldermen should also not be defensive in the matter of the police and the lottery. They should push ahead with a full-scale investigation, letting the chips fall, for only a bold thorough investigation would clear the chief and the other officers under suspicion. Anything less would be looked upon by the citizens as a whitewash. Any attack on the grand jury would be interpreted as criticism and should be avoided.

The mayor, his advisors suggested, might be wise to take the lead in sponsoring any grand-jury investigation, insisting on adequate funds and the hiring of a special high-calibre investi-gator who would do a thorough and objective study while at the same time protecting the interests of everyone concerned. (The mayor had always suspected that any criticism of his ad-ministration by a grand jury was the result of the grand jury's having been stacked with his political opponents or their em-ployees. On the other hand, the delivery to the grand jury of pictures showing the son of a grand juror in an embarrassing relationship with a girl in a downtown hotel was resented with equal fervor by the grand jurors. It was looked upon as an effort to intimidate them.)

Seeking advice from friends he trusted was the formal con-tinuation of an informal policy Hartsfield had been following since his first race for mayor in 1936. Then, when he had a plan or a problem in his mind, he would go and prowl the streets, buttonholing citizens, asking them what they would do if they were in his place. He would mull the answers over and make a decision based on what his unofficial "citizens' committee" had told him; that is, of course, if ideas coincided roughly with his own.

While Hartsfield's friends were advising him on ways to enhance his image, his enemies, and they were many, were casting about for an opponent who could beat him in the general election. Effort was made to get 2 percent of the registered voters to petition for the holding of a "Democratic" convention in September, at which a slate of candidates would be selected to run against Hartsfield and the other winners of the May primary. If such a convention could be set up, then strong effort would be made to draft Charlie Brown as its candidate for mayor—an honor Brown did not seem to welcome, since he had twice been beaten by Hartsfield already. Governor Marvin Griffin was also approached as a possible candidate.

Hartsfield of course denounced the effort as "a bunch of dejected and dissatisfied soreheads who are trying to find a way to bolt a perfectly fair primary in which every citizen had a chance to run and vote."[16] He then flew off to Mexico City for the inauguration of an Eastern Airline nonstop flight from New York to Mexico, which he hoped eventually would bring Aeronavis, the Mexican airline, to Atlanta.

In the long run it was neither Griffin nor Brown who challenged Hartsfield in the primary, but Lester Maddox, the restaurateur, beginning his own ill-starred run for the political roses. He went on television to denounce Hartsfield for his police policies, his domination of the city government, and his attitudes on racial matters. His own goal, Maddox said, was to throw out all those who would bring integration through force. Maddox said he would never sell *his* birthright to the NAACP.

Hartsfield had made known his views on race before a meeting of the Lion's Club, where he expressed the hope that Atlanta could continue to lead the South in peaceful progress toward understanding. "It is the white man who loses most when racial troubles erupt into violence," he said. "We do not want the hatred and bitterness of Montgomery or Little Rock." The way of violence, the way of dynamite, the way of hatred represented a "distinct loss" to white citizens, he said. "I'm not calling on anybody to surrender anything. I'm not trying to integrate anybody. I'm not trying to destroy traditions of the South. But no public official can do other than cling to the law." Hartsfield's views were more appealing to Atlantans than were those of Maddox. On December 4 Hartsfield's majority over Maddox was 41,000 to 23,000.

During the campaign several things had occurred to add strength to the Hartsfield cause. The October-November grand jury had investigated the charges against the police and had come out with a report which, Hartsfield felt, gave Chief Jenkins and his department a clean bill of health. *Fortune Magazine,* in its November issue, named Hartsfield as one of the nation's nine best mayors, and the *Atlanta Journal* in its endorsement said that though Hartsfield was not perfect, throughout the years he had stood for something—for physical progress, political progress—and by reelecting him the city would guarantee that its government would remain in honest hands, able to manage it in the interest of all its citizens.[17]

The *Constitution,* in its editorial rejoicing in Hartsfield's victory, sounded the first note of prophecy. "At the age of sixty-seven, the mayor may be embarking on his last term. We suggest that he has two great opportunities. He can needle the city government to greater progress, perhaps foregoing some of the usual political considerations. And he can start making room for the younger man who someday must succeed him."[18]

THE LAST LONG MILE

INDEED Hartsfield had been thinking of the years to come and the race that would be facing him four years hence when he would be seventy-one. Many things had come to pass in recent years that had set him thinking. While he was growing ever more powerful politically, more successful in all he tried to do for his civic family, the relationships with those closest to him personally had gone through a sad deterioration. Due in part to her failing eyesight and the increasingly poor health that had plagued her for all her seventy years, Pearl Hartsfield no longer stood with him at rallies and speeches, for her interests now were solely those of a housewife, mother, and grandmother, not a politician's wife.

Fannie Lee Bettis, who had been both secretary in his Grant Building office and friend and counselor in his lonely and troubled hours, was ill and dying now, after more than twenty years in his service. She was still much in his thoughts, though, for he was determined to show to her that loyalty she had shown to him, by taking care of all her financial needs in the years of her last illness. When she died at last, in 1958, at the age of fifty-four, he bought the headstone for her grave.

There was another person, too, whose friendship might have a bearing on his future. Even in his advancing years he had not lost his interest in beautiful, bright, warm and understanding women, and one of these, a widow with a little boy, had worked as a volunteer in his last two campaigns and had served as his unofficial hostess at social affairs. And somehow he knew that as long as he lived, in office or out, he would always want Tollie Tolan somewhere near him. But that would mean marriage. And in Atlanta, even in these times, a man in politics did not put by the wife to whom he had been married for forty-five years and take a wife who was only a few years more than half his age. And that was something he would brood on, day after day, as in January 1958 he went into his sixth term as mayor.

There was no sign of his personal concerns in his look or his voice as he spoke to the aldermanic board in its first session of the year. He traced the events of the past year briefly—the grand jury investigation which cleared the police department and its leadership, the fifty-one million dollars in bond issues, the completion of Buford Dam, the new feline house at Grant Park Zoo, the street improvements, and the creation of the Department of Urban Renewal. He outlined his plans for the year to come—new schools to be built with the bond money, new waterworks plants, and a new air terminal to be started. There were other things still needed—a public relations department, made up of people trained to tell the city's story, and an administrative assistant to take some of the daily burden off the mayor. More necessary than any of these, however, was action by the legislature to enable the city to levy taxes on values other than real estate. And above all else, the city must continue to move in the Atlanta way—toward the peaceful solution of all social and racial problems.[1]

Among those who knew Hartsfield and his determination in the past that he alone should rule his city, this campaign to create a director of public relations and an administrative assistant seemed to indicate that he was indeed beginning to weaken a little. He had long needed such help but refused to ask for it in the belief that to abdicate even a modicum of his power would not be wise politically. He was also careful to give no hint, outside his closest circle of advisors, that he might not run again in 1961. Nothing, he knew, could be lamer than a lame duck mayor. Nobody, he knew, would genuflect to a setting political sun.

For this reason, as well as his own inner compulsions, he kept swinging, right and left, throughout his term. He made open war, through the Georgia Municipal Association, on the county-unit system, which he denounced for giving the rural areas dominance over the municipalities, virtually disfranchising the city voter. Before audience after audience he called for all-out war on the system. He also set in motion a court suit to end it, a suit which after some setbacks and modifications, attorney Morris Abram was to take to the Supreme Court, where the system at last was outlawed. His attack on the county unit, plus his views on race, resulted in so many angry and insulting telephone calls that he wrote the telephone company, asking them to leave his home and Grant Building office number out of the next directory, if this could be done while still giving out the number to long-distance callers. This was atypical of the old Hartsfield, who wanted to be available at all times and in all places, to his city family.

Hartsfield's crusade against the county-unit system was matched by his all-out attack on the method of taxation permitted the cities by the legislature. Atlanta's merchants, Hartsfield argued, were the most effective tax-collecting agency in Georgia, for they nicked each Atlanta consumer for his sales tax. But it was the state, not the city, which got the money, and city services suffered.

Hartsfield's outraged reaction to the bombing of the Jewish Temple in Atlanta in October 1958 brought him national recognition. He went immediately to the scene and offered a thousand dollar reward, to be paid by the city, for information leading to the conviction of the bombers. He then ordered Police Chief Herbert Jenkins to go all-out in his investigation.

Hartsfield was convinced that the bombers were not Atlanta residents. "Rabble rousers have long been frustrated by the fact they couldn't start anything in Atlanta . . . Our homegrown rabble rousers have had to take their hate and trouble other places."[2]

He called on all decent people to rise up and denounce the bombers, blaming the dynamiting on the fact that so-called good citizens had been guilty of demagoguery. "Whether they like it or not every political rabble rouser is the god-father of these cross burners and dynamiters who sneak about in the dark and give a bad name to the South . . . One day it is a church, another it is a school. Unless it is checked it will be homes and business houses next."[3]

Always quick to see the hand of communism at work behind any untoward event, Hartsfield suggested that these dynamitings throughout the South could be masterminded by people having international motives, working through local dupes who fomented race hate and bigotry that hurt America in the eyes of the world.

A few days later Hartsfield received a letter from President Eisenhower: "By your swift and efficient efforts following last Sunday's wanton bombing of the Hebrew Benevolent Congregation, and by your forceful and unequivocal denunciation of this despicable act, you and your city administration have set an example for the entire nation."[4] He added his personal commendation and appreciation to Hartsfield and his police department.

Atlanta's reaction to the Temple bombing also inspired a profile of Hartsfield by Bob Greene in *Newsday*, describing him as the Dixie counterpart of New York's late Mayor LaGuardia, in that he liked to chase fire engines, prowl the streets in a police car, demand puritanical honesty from his police officers, and exercise almost stifling control over every department in his administration. Hartsfield's most amazing talent, said

Newsday, was his ability to turn a policy of racial moderation into a political asset—one of the few deep South politicians who could do this. Quoting Hartsfield's denunciation of "rabble-rousing politicians" as the godfathers of the crossburners and dynamiters, *Newsday* pointed out that such statements made Hartsfield's name anathema to rural Georgians but carried him back into office in Atlanta over a rabid segregationist. Citing some of Hartsfield's bold strokes—providing Ralph Bunche with a police escort because "he's a great American," desegregating the golf courses, and other incidents—*Newsday* described Hartsfield as being a man who would be looked upon as a moderate up North, but was known as a flaming liberal down South.[5]

The year drew to a close with Hartsfield and many of his supporters in Atlanta in bitter confrontation with Governor Griffin and the rest of the state. The issue was school integration. Since the school ruling in 1954 Georgia, and every other state in the South, had used every legal weapon in the book to avoid the "mixing" of white and black children in the schools. Each effort had failed. Time was running out and there was strong likelihood that the schools of Atlanta would be under order to integrate with the opening of the school year in September 1959. But Hartsfield had one more holding action up his sleeve. He asked the state legislature to allow Atlanta to hold a referendum in which the citizens themselves would decide what they wanted to do with their schools—integrate them, or close them. (Either way the city was trapped. If the schools were integrated under federal law, state law demanded that they be closed.)

Governor Griffin denounced Hartsfield. He was sure that Atlanta would accept black children rather than close the city's schools, and he was determined that this should not happen. "He can't throw in the towel for me," roared Griffin to an *At-*

lanta Journal reporter. Hartsfield replied that he was not throwing in any towels. He deplored the Supreme Court decision as much as anyone else. All he was asking was that each community be allowed to decide what to do about its own schools. The name-calling argument went on and on—with Governor-elect Ernest Vandiver adding his voice to that of Griffin. In such a contest Hartsfield was more than able to hold his own. In reply to Governor Griffin he said that if the governor had any real concern for Atlanta's citizens he would let them have the right to decide for themselves the fate of their own schools.

It was Hartsfield's good fortune that in this shouting match with the governor, he had strong moral support. Powerful forces had been quietly at work in Atlanta and throughout the state, bringing about a subtle change from defiance to reluctant acceptance of the idea that black and white could share the same schools without the heavens falling. In November 1957 eighty Atlanta ministers, representing all the major Protestant denominations, had come out with a far-reaching manifesto outlining their views on race relations. Believing that their statement would be helpful to all those who felt that "we must solve the race situation in love and on our knees," thousands of copies were sent out by the United Churchwomen of Atlanta and the executive committee of the United Churchwomen of Georgia. Their beliefs were these: That all Americans and churchmen have an obligation to obey the law; that whether or not an individual agrees with the 1954 school decision, he must abide by it until by legal process it might be changed. Above all, the public school system must not be destroyed.

All the town's leading preachers signed their names to this. To Hartsfield, a churchgoing Baptist and a leader of his congregation, there could be no stronger support. Nor did the ministers fire one salvo and then fall silent. The following year, when the row between Hartsfield and Governor Griffin was at its height, the ministers came out with another manifesto. This time, not 80 but 311 Atlanta clergymen supported Hartsfield's stand.

Many controversial items other than the school issue had furrowed Hartsfield's brow as his city moved on into the closing years of the fifties. He still was fighting the state, demanding the right for the city to levy a sales tax, or an employment tax, or a highway-use tax of its own, so that the tax burden on home-owners could be lightened. He and his lawyer, Morris Abram, were still pushing their anti–county-unit suit toward the Su-preme Court, bypassing one legal obstacle after another. The city's basis for asking the Supreme Court to rule on a matter of state legislation was Hartsfield's and Abram's argument that the school decision, directed against state laws, had set the precedent. If state laws could be struck down because they denied equal rights to school children, they could be struck down because they denied equal rights to voters.

His urban renewal program bogged down in mid-1958, sabo-taged, he claimed, by landlords—Judases, he called them—who for years had profited by a shortage of decent housing. To get it going again, Hartsfield went before the board of aldermen and in a two-hour harangue that caused some of the board to head quietly for the doors, he got it back on the tracks, laying the responsibility on the aldermen for its success.

Constant criticism of his police outraged him, and so did the limitation of the authority of city courts, which were required to bind over to county courts for trial those accused of even the most minor offense. Why should his police be constantly in-vestigated, he asked. Why should not a study be made of the defects of the judiciary, he demanded. County court judges, he argued, were neither holy nor sanctified and there should be some sort of citizens' supervision of their acts, to discover how many criminal cases were being postponed, and for how long, how many sentences were reduced, how many cases dead docketed, in the administration of what he called "horse-and-buggy, fodder pulling justice."[6]

His remarks were in reply to a story in *Time* magazine which said that Atlanta had the second highest crime rate in the United States. At Hartsfield's urging, J. Edgar Hoover wrote a letter to *Time* saying that the story had misinterpreted FBI figures. At the insistence of the police committee of his aldermanic board, he finally did appoint a "crime committee," made up of leading citizens and headed by Morris Abram, to study the crime situation in the Atlanta area and make its recommendations to the city, to Fulton and DeKalb grand juries, and to the legislature. He warned his appointees, however, that such a committee would inevitably attract "nuts, cranks, and people with axes to grind."[7]

A hint that Hartsfield's power possibly was diminishing had come in 1958, in the September elections to the state legislature, when two of his stalwart supporters, former senator G. Everett Millican and former representative Hamilton Lokey, were defeated by Charlie Brown and Wilson Brooks in their efforts to return to office. To many this meant that Hartsfield no longer dominated the local political scene. And this weakening, so the deep-down rumors ran, was the result of a growing belief among politicians that Hartsfield would not run for mayor again. This of course was true. Hartsfield by now had made up his mind. But he kept silent on his plans, and he gave no sign of any weakening as he went, with his usual buoyant enthusiasm, into his twenty-second year in City Hall.

In his address to the board of aldermen on January 6, 1959, he conjured up the ghost of Henry Grady. Atlanta, he said, was looked up to throughout the new and burgeoning South as the leader in the field of municipal progress. It was at the moment in the midst of one of the greatest civic and municipal renovation, enlargement, and improvement programs of any city in the nation, and nothing must impede this progress. "I appeal to you, as I do to all citizens, not to let the poison virus of hatred and discord get into our government. Let us be of good will to all, the high and the low, the rich and the poor, and people of every color, race or creed." "Atlanta," he said in conclusion, "has a good reputation all over the nation . . . Let us resolve regardless of temptation or abuse, to maintain the good reputation in years to come."[8]

Though deploring extremists and calling for calm in his official utterances, Hartsfield was quite willing to come out swinging, throwing verbal punches in his informal utterances. The new year was only three days old when he blasted anew at Georgia's politicians and pledged to continue the fight to keep state and city schools open. "I don't give a damn what [Governor] Griffin or anyone else said. I refuse to see Georgia go through another period of ignorance," he told the Northside Atlanta Kiwanis Club. "People have asked me why I got in this school fight and I'm not ashamed to tell you. I am the son of a father and mother who saw Reconstruction. Sherman's troops destroyed all that my father's family had. My father was in school when they were closed. He came to Atlanta ignorant and uneducated because they had no schools. I don't want to see another generation grow up under such a handicap."[9] Waving his arms, shouting hoarsely in a voice raspy with laryngitis, Hartsfield brought his audience of businessmen to their feet in a long standing ovation.

A few days later at the airport, Hartsfield and Alderman Jesse Draper, chairman of the aviation committee, climbed into the cab of a huge pile driver to have their pictures taken "officially" breaking ground for a new twelve-million-dollar airport terminal. The weather was cold, the ground like stone, the water lines in the pile driver were frozen, and no ground was broken that day. This gave the mayor a chance to gather the press around him in the office of Jack Gray, then the airport manager. There he reminisced of his first groundbreaking here thirty-five years earlier. The city, at Alderman Hartsfield's urging, had appropriated five thousand dollars to build an airport, and Hartsfield had come out with a newsreel photographer who took his picture posed behind a mule and a dirt scoop. The weather was warm, the mule's pipes were not frozen, and the first panful of dirt was moved.[10]

Hartsfield in 1959 was pushing not only for Atlanta's airport development but for federal aid to airfields nationwide. In Washington he told the senate aviation committee that he was speaking for thirteen thousand American towns and cities when he asked support for a bill that would provide $575 million in federal aid to airports in the next five years.

The desegregation without violence of Atlanta's buses and trolleys gave Hartsfield a chance again to defy the "clowns and demagogues" who had predicted riots and intermarriage if black and white riders were allowed to sit beside each other on the bus. He said he had no worries about Negroes causing "incidents" on buses because "Negroes have been taught since they were born to avoid incidents 365 days a year."[11]

After years of battling to annex Buckhead and finally succeeding, Hartsfield now sought to annex Sandy Springs, which was seeking adequate fire protection. Sandy Springs was not persuaded. At a meeting to discuss annexation Hartsfield was roundly booed and not permitted to speak. He shrugged the incident off, observing that if Sandy Springs didn't want Atlanta, Atlanta didn't want Sandy Springs. Sandy Springs continued to "not want" Atlanta through the administrations of Ivan Allen, Jr., Sam Massell, and Maynard Jackson.

Hartsfield, famed for his feuding with the Georgia legislature, found himself at odds with the two Atlanta members of the Fulton County delegation, Wilson Brooks and Ralph McClelland—so much so that when he made an impromptu visit to the house they asked him to get off the floor and quit embarrassing them before their fellow legislators. Hartsfield had gone over to ask them to approve a bill taking the ceiling off Atlanta's business licenses and to approve a bill that would put a ceiling on property taxes. The mayor, after a shouting match, left, alleging that he had been subjected to arrogant and churlish insults by Fulton County legislators who were using Atlanta as the helpless whipping boy of their hatred and spleen.[12]

The row between the mayor and the legislators ended in a lot of sound and fury, signifying nothing much beyond the fact that Brown, Brooks, and McClelland of the Fulton delegation didn't like Hartsfield, and Hartsfield didn't like them. It was, therefore, a matter of politics. In the long run, though, the mayor won the main bout. No ceiling was placed on city property taxes, which meant that the city would not go hungry for revenue in the future. As for the citizens of Sandy Springs— who stubbornly refused to be annexed and refused also to pay Atlanta for providing top-grade fire protection—they simply did not trust Atlanta.

SO LONG, OLD TIGER

Rows with antagonistic legislators over city taxes, with dentists over the threat of fluoridation, with Sandy Springs residents over annexation, with state officials who demanded that Atlanta should close her schools rather than integrate them, kept Hartsfield's temper at the boiling point as the decade of the fifties came to a close. Problems with his investments in oil and gas wells, in filling-station leases, motels, and coin laundries troubled him sorely. One event late in the year, however, caused him to glow with pride and happiness. On October 10, 1959 Atlanta, as Hartsfield had predicted, came to be a city of a million inhabitants—not all living within the city limits, of course, but in the metropolitan area. Messages poured in from mayors all over the world whom Hartsfield had met in his travels abroad; and the city, at his urging, held a joyful celebration at the auditorium, with forty-four mayors and commissioners from surrounding counties joining in. To commemorate this great event—and the past from which it sprang—the city printed billions of dollars in simulated million-dollar "Confederate" bills and distributed them throughout the country as an expression of its thanks for the real money that smart Yankees and Westerners had poured into the city in recent years. An article in *Newsweek* by Atlantan Bill Emerson, based largely on interviews with Hartsfield and the Atlanta Chamber of Commerce, indicated that in the last twenty years the metropolitan area had doubled, making Atlanta, next to Houston, Texas, the fastest growing metropolitan area in the United States.

These boom times corresponded closely with Hartsfield's five terms as mayor, and it was due, he said, to the city's still letting itself be guided by Henry Grady's philosophy of forgetting the past and getting to work. "We sail serenely on," said Hartsfield to Emerson, "with the demagogues picking at us, pulling our feathers, harassing us." He then made the statement from which one of his most famous quotes was derived:

We say we're too busy to hate—it's the pattern of modern Atlanta set by Henry Grady. Our life blood is communication, contact with the balance of the nation. We greatly yearn to be a part of the nation. We seethe under the fact that we are not held in high regard by either political party. We strive to undo the damage the Southern demagogue does to the South. We strive to make an opposite impression from that created by the loud-mouth clowns. Our aim in life is to make no business, no industry, no educational or social organization ashamed of the dateline "Atlanta."

Remember . . . the 14th Amendment guarantees Northern money equal treatment. The secret of our success—we roll a red carpet out for every damn Yankee who comes in here with two strong hands and some money. We break our necks to sell him.[1]

These "Yankees" came from everywhere. In 1958 only four states failed to contribute new citizens to Atlanta. From New York came 117 families and from Illinois 106. Frequently when branch managers had served a term in Atlanta, they refused to be transferred elsewhere. There were also families moving to Atlanta from Japan, Chile, Denmark, Formosa, and Syria—an influence which, along with the Yankee newcomers, brought, in Hartsfield's words, "a terrific infusion of enthusiasm, information, broadmindedness . . . liberality . . . and a constant search for ideas." During the 1950s under Hartsfield, said *Newsweek*'s correspondent, Atlanta was "crackling with life, vitality and dollars."[2]

The combination of ideas, energy, and dollars brought into being Ed Noble's Lenox Square, John Portman's Merchandise Mart, Mills Lane's new Commerce Building, and the building of many smaller structures which Hartsfield called Ben Massell's "one-man boom." One point that *Newsweek* strongly made, its reporter had learned from both Ben Massell and Ed Noble: in Hartsfield's Atlanta, there were no sticky-fingered city hall employees who had to be paid off before the proper permits could be issued.

While the new things were happening, Hartsfield was fond of pointing out, Atlanta's older bellwether businesses were going stronger than ever—Coca-Cola and Scripto pencils pushing into all corners of the world, the Lovable Brassiere Company and Delta Airlines expanding to meet growing demands for uplift and airlift.

The arrival of her millionth citizen in Hartsfield's view represented a challenge to the city that every new arrival would intensify. For all its progress, one-fourth of Atlanta's million still lived in substandard housing; though urban renewal was helping to make a dent in white and black slums alike, much slum property still represented valuable investments for the few and misery for the many. There was less tension between the races than in any other city in the South, but the school integration problem still cast its dark shadow upon the city. And above all, there was no plan for the orderly development of the metro area across county lines, or within them. Old mistakes were being made over again and new slums created, though Fulton County, through its Metropolitan Planning Commission, and DeKalb County to a lesser degree were moving ahead with faith and optimism toward a happier more orderly future.

All these things were on Hartsfield's mind as he appeared before his board of aldermen to outline his plans for 1960. Closest to his heart were the schools, and he made an eloquent plea for the support of open schools, publicly supported. He knew, he said, that the people of Atlanta, proud of their city, its marvelous growth and good reputation, would rise to the challenge, opposing "those who will as usual shout hatred and confusion . . . I therefore urge that the entire city government and all our citizens in every walk of life place themselves squarely behind the preservation of public education and make the same known to the members of the Georgia legislature."

The closing of the schools, he argued, would bring Atlanta's progress to a halt. "It will do little good to bring about more brick, stone and concrete, while a shocked and amazed world looks at a hundred thousand innocent children roaming the streets."[3] Another plan to which Atlanta's progress was deeply tied, he pointed out, was more urban renewal, to solve the problems of downtown blight and to increase and improve living quarters for both black and white. New auditoriums were needed, new stadiums, new parks and recreational facilities. In this talk, two decades before rapid transit became a reality, he foresaw and urged the creation downtown of traffic tunnels and the use of existing rail lines in a system that was to become known as MARTA.

In 1959 the city had built a five-hundred-thousand-dollar primate house, one of whose inhabitants was a baby gorilla, bought by the city for forty-five hundred dollars and promptly called "Willie B." by the zoo attendants. Hartsfield, with his fine flair for publicity, knew that Willie B.'s appeal to the general public would to a great degree overcome the criticism heaped upon him by his political opponents for spending so much money housing monkeys.

Politics was much on the public mind at the moment, though the next mayor's race was still a year away. As early as September 1959 Ed Hughes, *Journal* city hall reporter, headlined his "City Beat" column MAYOR WILL RUN IF HE CAN WALK. And from Hartsfield's public actions and statements it seemed that he would indeed try to stay in City Hall forever. But Hartsfield by now, for political as well as personal reasons, was thinking of making a complete change in his life's pattern. He not only wanted a new job; he wanted a new family. The political decision, though, had to be made first.

From George Goodwin, a friend with a talent for interpreting election returns, he had learned some disturbing news. In the 1957 election against Lester Maddox, Maddox had gotten the majority of the white vote. To Hartsfield this meant that there had been a temporary break in the alliance that had sent him into the mayor's office five times in a row—the old understanding between City Hall, the town's top business leaders, and the newspapers. With a little effort he felt he could mend these broken fences again. To Goodwin, a shrewd observer of Atlanta politics, the problems went deeper than that. In the years since the war many rural Georgians had moved to Atlanta, bringing with them ideas, particularly on race, that Hartsfield did not share. To these country-bred newcomers Hartsfield, with his talk of open schools, was a dangerous man. There was also a growing feeling that the old mayor was letting his temper run away with him too often. "Some of our friends," said Goodwin, "are taking the line that 'Old Bill has become irascible and has made a lot of enemies. If we had someone who thought like him but didn't act like him, we'd have no trouble.' "[4]

Hartsfield was a proud man—proud of his city, proud of the part he had played in making it what it was—and the prospect of running for mayor at the age of seventy-one and of being beaten by some young squirt—or what was worse by one of his old enemies—did not appeal to him. So plans long forming in his mind began to take concrete shape. Early in March 1960 Pearl Williams Hartsfield, his wife for forty-seven years, wrote their daughter, Mildred, in Macon, telling her that the mayor had asked her to give him a divorce. He wanted her to file the suit, charging mental cruelty, and he promised that it would all be handled very quietly by his lawyers, on the basis of mutual agreement. Mrs. Hartsfield was well aware that his feelings toward her had changed since their courting days. Then, he would write her tender and impassioned love letters, and when in a fit of jealousy he said something that had hurt her, he would abjectly apologize, promising that once they were married it would never happen again. She got out these old love letters and read them over. "I know I am given to talking like that at times but if you will just help me I know I won't be that way any more . . . When you started crying this evening it came over me in a second how mean I had been to you . . . Would you believe me when I say that I'd rather have my tongue cut out than to talk to my precious little wife that way."[5]

She looked again at the pictures he had taken, with a delayed-action camera, of the two of them after their marriage, walking in the park, riding in a buggy, working together in the kitchen of their first home, which had burned in the great Atlanta fire of 1917. She read over again a letter he had written to their son, William, Jr., on his second birthday:

My dear little Man: . . . Just two years ago you were a little mite of humanity, all cuddled up in flannels, in a darkened room, lying beside your proud but tired little mother. Papa was standing over you and put his finger in your hand and your little fingers closed around it and held it right tight. I shall never forget that. And do you remember how you tried to strangle yourself and how mama cried about it. My, but those were eventful days.

Your little life has been the source of untold happiness to Mama and Papa. Not only that, but it has been a liberal education to us both,—we have learned and will continue to learn almost as much as you. To watch you grow and develop is like the budding and unfolding of a beautiful little flower. All our hopes and ambitions are centered in you, and it is our one and only desire that time may bring them into full realization . . . Affectionately, Papa.

And time did bring the budding and unfolding of a bright mind and a courageous spirit. William Berry Hartsfield, Jr., turned out to be an excellent student, making a brilliant record at Commercial High, where he displayed his father's flair for shorthand and typing, and later at Georgia Evening College, where he taught. In time, though, illness—asthma and Bright's disease, and what doctors believed to be the tension of striving to live up to the expectations of a famous father—brought on health problems that were overcome only after years of struggle.

Pearl Hartsfield was seventy-five years old in 1960. Her health was failing and she was almost blind. She had long been aware that their marriage had become meaningless, that she had become no more than a housekeeper to the mayor. But there had been no inkling that this arrangement had become intolerable to him. Over the years there had often been harsh words between them, mainly over money, for Hartsfield's business interests kept him strapped for household funds. But there had been no sudden quarrel, no unusually bitter argument, to presage a final break.

She told him, therefore, that after all these years of marriage she had no desire to sue him for divorce. If he wanted to end their marriage he would have to bring the suit himself and provide a financial settlement adequate to take care of her in her last years. This answer caused some problems. Hartsfield, as usual, was short of resources, and the series of financial settlements he offered, one after the other, were rejected by Mrs. Hartsfield and by her daughter, Mildred, who was acting as advisor to her mother. And Hartsfield was also well aware that if he did go to court, suing on the grounds of mental cruelty, Mrs. Hartsfield would no doubt have a great deal to say about who had been mentally cruel to whom. And this, he knew, would be the end of him politically.

All these things were turning over in his mind when early in 1961 Helen Bullard called on him at City Hall to ask about his plans for the mayor's race that fall. She had been Hartsfield's political mentor for twenty years, and her loyalty to him was complete. But now Ivan Allen, civic leader and son of a distinguished Atlantan, wanted to run and wanted her to help him. She had five thousand dollars in her purse. "It's from Ivan," she told Hartsfield. "He says to tell you if you are going to run again, it's a campaign contribution to help you get started. But if you are not going to run, he wanted to know it as soon as possible, so he can make his own plans." Hartsfield went over and stood by the window, looking out over the city. When he turned back, there were tears in his eyes. He handed the money back to her. "Tell Ivan to come to see me," he said.[6]

Allen went a few days thereafter. Hartsfield kept him waiting for more than an hour, and then, when Allen finally was admitted to his office, he paced the floor for forty-five minutes, Allen recalled, complaining about the hardships of being mayor, the endless papers to be signed, the difficulties of working with aldermen who preferred playing golf to looking after the city's business. It was a pattern that had become routine with him, this long and angry harangue of anybody who came to see him, no matter what their mission.

Finally he wound down, and Allen got a chance to ask his question. In his book, *Mayor,* Allen recalls the scene: "I think you can be elected," he told Hartsfield. "I'll put ten thousand dollars in your campaign fund and take a leave of absence from my company so I can be your campaign manager. I can help you with younger people, and you can be elected." Hartsfield said, "You wouldn't make an offer like that unless you wanted something, now, would you?" "No, sir," Allen said. "If you are *not* going to run, I'd like for you to make an announcement so that the rest of us can get in the race." Then, Allen recalls,

He went over to the window and stood there for a few minutes, mumbling to himself as the afternoon light played over his tired hulking frame and accented the wrinkles on his hands and neck. When he turned around he sounded like a very old, very tired man. "I've had this job for twenty-three years," he said. "I'm seventy-two years old, and I've been married for forty-eight of 'em, and now I'm in love with a very wonderful young lady and I want to marry her. I can't get a divorce and be re-elected mayor. If you'll send Helen Bullard over here tomorrow, I'll make my announcement and get out of the race so you boys can go on about your business. I've been around long enough."[7]

The next morning, June 7, 1961, at ten o'clock, he stepped out of his office to face the glare of movie cameras and to announce to the crowd of reporters that he would not be a candidate in the forthcoming primary. It was an emotional moment for the many old friends who had gotten the word of what was coming and had come to share it with him. They burst into prolonged applause.

"They seemed to realize," wrote Joe Cumming in *Atlanta* magazine, "that they were witnessing the farewell of the one man most responsible for bringing their town to its envied position of prosperity and leadership among all Southern cities —for making it a proud beautiful city . . . of new buildings rising in the clear sunlight, of fountains and bells at noon and flowers in parks created out of dismal patches of municipal wasteland."[8]

It was a sentimental moment, but its central figure did not choose to go the route of the moist eye, the catch in the throat. Wrote Cumming: "He stood erect, his face glowing with health which made him look younger than his 71 years. . . . And he talked simply, in his low-pitched, life-cracked voice—talked of his town, of the years gone and the days and years ahead."

At last his statement was over, and he stood there, a man of many moods and facets, a public figure with an inner private personality that made him an enigma to even his closest friends —a mature man with the serenity of a philosopher and the temper of a three-year-old child. And at times the ebullience of a teenager. As he finished his statement and the crowd began to drift away he grabbed the mike and bellowed into it: "The Undefeated Champ!"

Even while Hartsfield was uttering this last triumphant cry, the first edition of the *Atlanta Journal* was rolling with a story that tried to catch the essence of the man. "He's got a hot temper, a stinging tongue, a strong will, a quick wit, a kind heart, a sense of history, a sense of destiny, a sense of humor, a capacity for growth, and a built-in finely tuned political radar set that seldom has failed him in his public life," read the *Journal* story.[9]

And editor Eugene Patterson was turning out the masterful editorial tribute that appeared the next morning in the *Atlanta Constitution:*

So long, Bill.

You've done a great job. We know, you're still mayor and the hardest parts are yet to come. But just to hear your announcement, finally, that you don't intend to run forever makes us feel like saying "so long" in advance. That way we can say some nice things about you now.

About the nicest thing about you was the way you would come barging into the editor's office, sail your hat across the room and cuss us out with that fine, feigned fury that never quite concealed a cold, ordered mind. You were always at your best when you were wrong.

And brother, could you be wrong!

But mainly, we have to admit, you were right. You were mighty right about this town. You understood her. She's not just a big brute of a concrete settlement. She has strength, heart, soul, honor and beauty. You gave her all of that. Plaza Park, the airport, a monkey house with sculpture on it, blossoms in pots in the middle of Marietta Street—little parts of a big beauty . . .

You made Atlanta something more than Marthasville, Bill. She believes in a decent regard for the opposite race and the opposite point of view. She believes in culture, in education, in compassion and vigor. She's a part of the world. You were a key man in making her what she is. You rode her streets alone at night to watch over her sleep. You sat at her political bedside on Saturdays and Sundays while the rest of us sat on our patios. You fought mighty battles for her, and gave her voice.

Years later, at the March of Dimes ball in 1952, he treads a romping measure with another movie star, Helen Hayes.

Courtesy of the Woodruff Library, Emory University

His proudest moment. Hartsfield and his daughter Mildred (right) leave the Georgian Terrace with Clark Gable and Carole Lombard, bound for the *Gone with the Wind* ball, 1939.

Margaret Mitchell and Mayor Hartsfield commissioning the cruiser *Atlanta*, December 3, 1944.

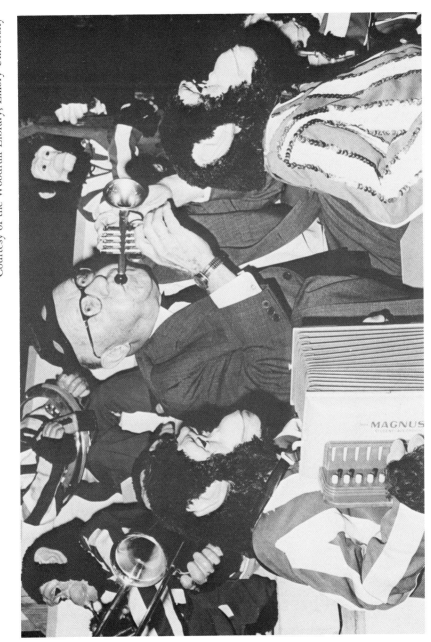

The mayor emeritus and the Monkey Band, Southeastern Fair, September 1966. He'd do anything for a laugh . . .

Courtesy of the Woodruff Library, Emory University

PLANES

Photo by Billy Downs; courtesy of the Woodruff Library, Emory University

. . . or a picture that would make the papers. Here
he leaps to touch Julian Harris's controversial airport mobile, 1967.

So when we hear you aren't going to run again, we think, well, it's going to take a mighty good man to carry on the pace you set.

And we wonder how it's going to be without that hat of yours sailing through the door and you following it in, all bug-eyed with rage, because we simply pointed out that you were wrong.

So long, old tiger.[10]

Business leaders across town were answering their telephones and framing up reaction quotes for reporters—quotes that spoke of "the end of an era" and said "he will leave mighty big shoes to fill." Not only the local papers but the national press made clear just how big those shoes had been and what a many-mooded man had worn them. Even as his days as mayor drew to a close, and personal problems bore heavily upon him, Hartsfield kept his political wits about him, concerned about his city and its image to the last. In the fall of 1960 when the sit-ins began in Atlanta, it was Hartsfield who worked night and day to keep them as peaceful and quiet as possible. When Martin Luther King was arrested when his party tried to be served at Rich's rooftop restaurant, Hartsfield knew that the time had come for the dramatic gesture. After conferring with Morris Abram, he hit upon a masterstroke of politics that had both local and national overtones. John F. Kennedy was campaigning somewhere in the West, and Hartsfield was unable to reach him. But certain that Kennedy would approve his action, he announced that candidate Kennedy had asked him to free Martin Luther King from his jail sentence. The word went all over the nation, and as Hartsfield knew he would, Kennedy, when he learned of it, did approve.

Hartsfield had a particular admiration for Kennedy. "There was quality there," he said. "There was quality in that whole family . . . and I sort of worship quality anyway—we've got so little of it. I'm in favor of the uncommon man myself."[11]

Hartsfield was soon to prove himself a man of uncommon

quality for a southern mayor as, in one of his last acts in office, he and Chief Herbert Jenkins in September 1961 carried out peacefully and quietly the integration of Atlanta's schools. Of all his many achievements—the airport, the Plan of Improvement, Hurt and Plaza parks—this was the one that in years to come would give him the greatest sense of satisfaction. It was a satisfaction well deserved. In Little Rock and New Orleans, court-ordered integration had taken place against a background of howling mobs. At the University of Georgia in Athens, Charlayne Hunter and Hamilton Holmes in January 1960 had been admitted, under court order, and again the cameras had shown rowdy demonstrators howling in protest. Hartsfield was determined that Atlanta, when her time came, should make no such ugly television spectacle of herself. She would instead stand out before the nation and the world as a shining example of wisdom and tolerance in bringing about social change. To accomplish this, though, would take some preparation. Word reached Chief Jenkins that troublemakers from all over the country would be coming to Atlanta as September neared, swelling the city's already ample collection of Klansmen, bombers, and assorted roughnecks. Carefully Hartsfield and Jenkins laid their plans. Detectives kept known hoodlums and crackpots under surveillance; gun merchants and sellers of commercial explosives were given pictures of all suspects who might be in the market for pistols and dynamite.

Four formerly all-white high schools were to be integrated by the admission of nine black students, and a police task force was set up to guard each school, keeping away every white person not actually working there. In addition a reserve force was held in standby at police stations, ready to move in a hurry to any school where trouble might break out.

Hartsfield, meanwhile, was making his own plans. He called a meeting of all the Atlanta media—newspapers, radio, and television—and laid down the ground rules. Stay out of the school buildings, he told them. If rioting broke out stay out of the way of the police. Photograph and record or report anything they saw or heard, but try to make it as nearly as possible a normal school day. He ordered Howard Monroe, his building superintendent at City Hall, to set up a pressroom there for the more than two hundred reporters who by now were pouring in from papers and wire services that covered the nation and the world. At Hartsfield's urging, Jenkins and John Letson, superintendent of schools, went on the air to urge parents and all Atlantans to accept the inevitable. Hartsfield himself made a fervent plea that the law be quietly obeyed, that integration be made to work. Jenkins assured parents that their children would come to school in safety, that his men were ready and could handle anything that might arise. He had seen to it that his men knew the meaning of what they were doing. All of the men had been through a special seminar in school integration where they had read books and heard lectures on the history of the movement and the court decisions they would be defending. Basically, Jenkins had told them, they would be answering one question. Should a bunch of hoodlums be allowed to destroy the system of public education in Atlanta?

The day came. The police took their places. The children arrived. The cameras whirred; the reporters scribbled in their notebooks, recording the fact that the historic day was much like any other opening day of school in Atlanta.

Hartsfield, with nearly three hundred out-of-town reporters in his city, could not resist putting on the type of public-relations show of which he was a master. He had the reporters driven from school to school, looking for the violence that never happened. That afternoon, after the school day ended without incident, he chartered a bus for all who wished to go and hauled the visiting journalists around the city. He drove them past some fine homes, calling out the names of the Negro businessmen, lawyers, bankers, and physicians who lived in these places. He took them past more modest, but still handsome, homes where Negro teachers and smaller merchants lived. He just wanted the visitors to know, he said, that the black people of Atlanta were making a real contribution to the city's growth and progress. They did not all live in shacks and hovels, but in houses equal to those in which the white folks lived.

That night he gave a cocktail party at the Biltmore Hotel for the visiting newsmen, some of whom were black. He told them that he knew how they felt. They were disappointed that they had come all this way for nothing. Then he added, with a grin that made his face light up, "But this is one time I'm truly proud you did not get the story you came to get." He did not feel it necessary to point out the fact that black and white journalists were sipping cocktails together in an Atlanta hotel, which was itself a landmark in the city's history.

All through 1961, while carrying out the official duties from which he would soon be free, his private thoughts were on the pressing matter of persuading "Miss Pearl" to give him freedom from the marriage that had endured for nearly fifty years. The wrangle over a settlement went on for months, with Mildred Hartsfield Cheshire representing her mother's interests with the zeal of a trained lawyer. It was a time of agony for her. She was proud of her father's achievements as mayor and of all the honors he had earned. Some of the high moments in her own life had been while in his company, playing the public role that her mother had long since given up.

But she loved her mother, and her brother, and was determined to protect them. In interview after interview with her father she stubbornly insisted that he could afford to pay far more than the $350 a month that he originally had offered. Sometimes in these arguments her father would become so provoked that he would fly into a rage, shouting and swearing, and in an effort to control himself, clenching his fist and biting it until it bled. Finally, though, a settlement was reached. Hartsfield was to give his wife $50,000 in cash, the house on Pelham Road, his son's medical expenses, a paid-up $10,000 insurance policy, and $300 a month for as long as she lived or until she married again. The divorce papers charging mental cruelty were filed by Hartsfield on November 3, 1961—less than a month after Ivan Allen had won his race for mayor. It was granted by Judge Virlyn B. Moore in his chambers on February 9, 1962 and was recorded on February 20.

On January 2, 1962, Hartsfield had made his last report to the board of aldermen with whom he had engaged in a love-hate relationship for so long. As usual he began his report with a prideful reference to the city's progress: "Again we have maintained an unparalleled record for cash operation, borrowing nothing for current operating expenses, winding up the year with all bills paid—and a cash carryover of $3,589,556.94, the largest in the history of our town."

He was proud, he said, to turn over to his successor so strong and healthy a city. He listed with equal pride other accomplishments of the past year—the dedication of the new twenty-million-dollar air terminal, the building of an observation tower in Grant Park, and the creation there of "beautiful new bear pits and a seal pool." "Most certainly," he went on,

we have met the challenge of a growing and dynamic city. About all of these things, we can be truly proud. But after all, they concern only money, manpower and material matters. A real city, in the truest meaning of the word, does not live by these things alone. Accordingly, we have tried to lend support to the cultural affairs of our city—to the performing arts, to exhibitions and good musical entertainment; to the establishment of good places to dine out, to a bright and decent night life, all of which means so much in the attraction of good citizens from elsewhere, and indirectly influences the location of many businesses in our town. A part of this is the new Merchandise Mart, which had the support of the city government, and which itself is a generator of more visitors and more businesses.

We have tried to make our city attractive to those from other parts of the nation having both money to invest and plants to build. It has paid off, both with an influx of new citizens and investments. Atlanta's growing downtown is silent witness to the soundness of our effort to maintain a strong central city, and to attract here the kind of folks who will contribute to our future growth.

But the most important thing about our city, with its natural advantages, as the great southern regional capital and center of southeastern trade and commerce, is its good name and its image before the balance of the nation. In this electronic and jet age, no place, no people, and no set of officials can escape the eye and ear of the balance of the world. Nor can they escape their responsibilities as citizens of that world.

Science has made all men neighbors, and as such they must find a way to live in peace and without hatred. Great decisions have been made in this field, decisions which have run counter to man of the habits and customs of the old South. Many sections of our southland have tried to stop the inexorable clock of time and progress, but without success and at great cost to themselves.

Atlanta's mature and friendly approach to the problems of racial change has earned for us the respect of the nation. Our leadership has enabled others in the South to do likewise. As the great branch office and regional center of the south, Atlanta's nerves and blood vessels extend all over the nation. To have adopted any other course than racial progress and harmony would have been doubly tragic for us, and a serious blow to our National Government in its fight to stave off world Communism.

Atlanta's peaceful school desegregation before the eyes of the whole nation was our finest hour. Our great airport terminal, which is our front door, and open to all, regardless of race, color or creed, is evidence to the world of the fact that here is a city which means to be a proud part of the great nation which we must support. Regardless of our personal feelings or past habits, we are living in a changing world, and to progress, Atlanta must be a part of that world.

He ended with the now familiar story of Atlanta as he found it in 1937, a little city covering only 37 square miles of land, three million dollars in debt and with a tax digest of only $350 million, compared to the city he was leaving to Mayor Allen—

138 square miles, with a million people in the metro area, and soundly financed by a tax digest of over one billion dollars.

And last came his tribute to his fellow workers and to the people of Atlanta: "For the balance of my life, I will be everlastingly grateful to them for their confidence and support. And now to the administration of Mayor Ivan Allen, President Sam Massell, and the newly constituted Board of Aldermen, . . . we present to you a city in good condition, with a clean shield. Thank you, and God bless our Atlanta."

This farewell was delivered in the flower-banked aldermanic chamber, in the evening after a long and busy last day spent in carrying out his final duties as mayor. Pat Watters, *Atlanta Journal* reporter, spent this day with him, recorded its activities, and concluded: "Then . . . the pretty girls pinned flowers on him, and people gushed over him, but I believe he enjoyed the last day better than the last night because right up until the speech, he was in charge, and responsible—for everything."[12]

Though he knew his political sun had set, Hartsfield's pride in his own achievement and his strong feeling for his city's future led him to sit down and prepare a memo for the guidance of his successor, Ivan Allen. It was blunt and to the point. First, he warned Allen to beware of the members of the county delegation in the legislature who were opposed to Atlanta, and the members of the county commission, who felt the same way. He went on:

The worst thing that has happened to the friendly City and County relationship was the death of Carlyle Fraser. It was he who stopped the County from picking on the City, unfriendly legislation, etc. As you know, those now in charge of the County were bitter enemies of the Plan of Improvement. Now that Fraser is dead, I am afraid they are going back into the business of City hating, trying to introduce legislation putting the County back into the City business, insisting on unfair contracts, etc.

Believe me, Ivan, this business of protecting the corporate City from unfair impositions by the suburbs is the most important thing you can do, and it will require some fighting and making yourself occasionally unpopular with the suburban areas.

If I were asked to give the greatest service I rendered during my entire reign, I would say it was the general policy of protecting corporate Atlanta from unfair tax situations, unfair contracts, getting the County out of the City business, generally stopping the overall arrangement by which the suburbs seek to live off of revenue collected in downtown Atlanta, and also by stopping efforts to weaken Atlanta's sovereignty and to get it into activities which should be assumed by a broader tax base.

A Stadium is fine, but it should be financed in some way as not to put the burden on the corporate taxpayer. This expanding, dynamic City has too many other needs out of its present Bond capacity. Likewise, a start towards a new Transit System is fine, but the central City should dominate it. We do not want to get in the shape of Boston, which submitted to a Transit Authority designated to the suburbs, who in turn kept low fares, with Boston paying the bill, a City which was forced to finance its own destruction. Incidentally, Boston is a classic example of a City completely hemmed in by dominant suburbs. When this happens, downtown will wither and die and we want to avoid it in Atlanta.

The most important thing you can do in your four years is to preserve Atlanta as a dominant central City, keep the suburbs from running it or trying to live off of its central area taxes, and also in developing some form of revenue paid by all of the people who use Atlanta, instead of by those whose property lies within the corporate limits . . .

Believe me, these things will require you to take firm stands and to be criticized for them, but they are basic to Atlanta's future prosperity.[13]

A SHOWMAN TO THE LAST

So spoke Hartsfield, strong-minded, belligerent, an "Old Tiger" to the end. Now he was free at last—free of official obligations to the city that had been his one true family, free too of the family by blood and marriage, which he could never bring himself to serve with the same fervor and devotion. There was more than idle boasting in his words to newspaper friends that he was not, at seventy-two, a doddering old man. His divorce became final on February 20, 1962. On July 11 of that year he married his beloved Tollie, Mrs. Tollie B. Tolan of Athens, Georgia. It was a surprise ceremony at the home of mutual friends, Dr. and Mrs. Thomas J. Harrold, in the little town of Winterville, near Athens, where Dr. Harrold was a professor at the university. To the beaming groom it was a wonderful day and a wonderful world. To the bride it was a somewhat hectic experience. Hartsfield had shown up at her house that morning, bringing her a purple-throated white orchid and telling her "today's the day." They had known each other for nearly a dozen years by now, and she was used to his impetuous, sometimes imperious ways. So she hastily scurried about, aided by a close friend, Mrs. Ruben Gotesky, getting her trousseau together, and at nine o'clock that evening, with Dr. Harrold standing as best man, they were joined in matrimony by Dr. Howard T. Giddens, pastor of the First Baptist Church in Athens. Hartsfield, Tollie remembered, was particularly pleased to be married by a Baptist.

The morning after the wedding they flew to New York on their honeymoon; first stop, Tiffany's, where Tollie picked out her diamond wedding ring. She picked the least expensive one, she recalls, for she was still feeling "kind of shy" with him. Their next stop was at the office of Jim Farley, head of The Coca-Cola Export Corporation, who had been asked by friends with The Coca-Cola Company in Atlanta to provide theater tickets for Hartsfield and his bride. Tollie went alone to Farley's office and as he handed her the tickets, he asked, "You are his daughter, aren't you?" "No," she said, "I'm his wife." "My God," said Farley, "Don't tell me he married a child!"

In finally making the long-delayed decision to divorce Pearl Hartsfield and marry Tollie, Hartsfield probably for the first time in his career went against the advice of his closest friend and most valued counselor, Robert Woodruff. When he first mentioned the idea, Woodruff, with characteristic bluntness, told him he was a fool to consider such a thing. It wouldn't work. He cited some of their aging Atlanta contemporaries who had married younger women, with unhappy results. At his age, said Woodruff, Hartsfield would soon be needing a nurse far more than he would need a young wife.

This did not represent, on Woodruff's part, any aversion to Tollie, whom he knew and liked. It did represent certain traditional ideas that he held about the enduring qualities of a marriage. In this case, though, Hartsfield knew his own mind and heart better than anyone else, and in the long run his decision proved, for him at least, to be the right one. The years he spent with Tollie in the little house he bought for her on Stovall Boulevard were the happiest of his long life. They traveled to far places, they went to the symphony and the theater together. He had complained in earlier days that if he wanted to go to any cultural event with a companion, he had to take an alderman along (usually Muggsy Smith). They entertained at home, at the Commerce Club, and at the Capital City Club, where Hartsfield had been given a life membership; Tollie presided as hostess at these events with charm and grace and a sometimes antic wit. He was particularly pleased that she shared his love for music and worked for the symphony, and he was equally glad that she shared his straitlaced Baptist principles. Neither liked to dance or play cards, and he once told her he was happy that she did not want to be active in politics. Women active in the League of Women Voters, he told her, were frustrated.

Hartsfield was only two years younger than Tollie's own father, whom he referred to jovially as "the Old Man," but Woodruff's prediction that he needed a nurse far more than he needed a wife half his age proved premature. Hartsfield retained his vigor, his zest for living, until his last days, and despite the disparity in their ages—he was seventy-two, she, forty—their private life was happy and fulfilling for them both.

Hartsfield, a self-educated man, was proud of the fact that Tollie had graduated from college and sometimes in gatherings of scholars would announce amiably that *his* education was in his wife's name. Born Tollie Bedenbaugh in Athens in 1922, she had finished Athens High School in 1939 and the University of Georgia, where she majored in home economics, in 1943. She taught for four years and then, looking for something more exciting, moved to Atlanta to take a job as a research assistant at Georgia Tech. There she met and married a young ex-Marine, an engineering student named Dan Tolan. Needing more money, she got a job in the personnel department at City Hall, finishing second in her tests out of three hundred applicants. There she first met the mayor, who, on looking over the educational requirements for various city jobs, announced with a certain rueful humor that the only job at City Hall for which *he* could qualify was that of mayor.

Hartsfield's lack of formal education often revealed itself in his mispronunciation of words and occasionally his enthusiasm caused him to lapse into humorous malapropisms. Tollie recalls his standing up at an opera finale once, shouting, "Brayvo, Brayvo, Author, Author," causing her to remind him gently that the proper pronunciation was "Brah-vo," and that Wagner or Bach, or whoever, was long since dead.

As Tollie Hartsfield remembers it, she was not greatly impressed by the mayor when they first met. She had seen a movie about Huey Long, which had left her with an innate distrust of all politicians. Even when continued acquaintance made her realize that Hartsfield was neither dishonest, crooked, nor evil, and was in fact an excellent mayor, her civil service job at City Hall forbade her working in his campaign.

When her husband Dan graduated in physics from Georgia Tech, they moved to Evansville, Indiana, where they adopted a little boy, Carl Siegfried; later the family moved to Florida. The marriage grew shaky, and there was a divorce. Soon though it was discovered that Dan Tolan had leukemia, and at his and his parents' request, he and Tollie went back together. They moved back to Atlanta for Dan's treatments and what proved to be the long process of dying. Once back in Georgia the relationship between the young people and the mayor grew closer. When Tollie would go to visit Dan in Emory Hospital, Hartsfield would sit with young Siegfried. (Soon after he and Tollie were married, Hartsfield adopted the boy, and almost as if to compensate for the fact that he had failed to establish a close relationship with his own son, he paid the youngster a great deal of attention. He insisted that he be known as "Carl." The name "Siegfried," he explained, would be a handicap if he should ever decide to go into politics in the South.)

Dan Tolan died in 1960, leaving Tollie with her young baby, and it was soon thereafter that Hartsfield began to tell her, seriously, that he wanted to marry her. "I wasn't sure I wanted to," Tollie Hartsfield recalled years later. "We had lots of discussions. He would say, 'People who want to be together ought to be,' and that was a strong argument. It was a tremendous love affair that happens once in a lifetime, and you wake up in the middle of the night scared to death, thinking that you could have missed it . . . I told him that if anybody ever asked why I married him, I would say they ought to have heard his campaign speeches."[1]

This courtship went on for two years, with Tollie coming over from Athens to serve as his unofficial hostess at a number of public functions. She was present at the dedication of the new Atlanta airport terminal in 1961 and was present at the cocktail party that he gave for the press following the peaceful desegregation of the schools. The mayor, Tollie discovered, would sometimes come over to Athens, unannounced, and drive up and down past her house on Broad Street, as nearly half a century before he had kept a jealous eye on the boardinghouse where Pearl Williams lived.

Since Hartsfield was giving up his job as mayor, and in his divorce settlement had agreed to give his first wife nearly all his assets, Tollie, with a child to raise and educate, was naturally interested in how he was going to make a living. "He told me, 'Don't worry about that,' " she said. " 'I took care of my parents. I've taken care of everybody. I can take care of you.' "[2]

And he did. Hartsfield in his years as mayor had built up a tremendous amount of goodwill and respect among institutions whose officers recognized that nobody could be a more effective advisor and consultant on how to do business in Atlanta. Therefore he soon found himself on retainer from The Coca-Cola Company, the Trust Company of Georgia, the Georgia Power Company, and for a while he was an editorial commentator on WSB television. These fees, with his six-thousand-dollar-a-year pension from the city and a new twelve-thousand-dollar-a-year job which soon was to come along, gave him an income of some sixty-thousand dollars a year, which was more than he had earned as mayor. (Now and then he also got an unexpected windfall. Occasionally Bob Woodruff would put Hartsfield, along with others of Woodruff's less affluent friends and associates, into a stock syndicate. When the stock went up, it was sold. Hartsfield and the others divided the profits, and Woodruff got his money back, to be used again. Since the market was rising and Woodruff was unerring in his ability to pick a winner, Hartsfield's share might amount to several thousand dollars.)

His new job was tailor-made for Hartsfield's talents as a showman. Elfred S. Papy, an Atlanta businessman who had been president of the Southeastern Fair Association since 1954, retired in February 1962, just a month after Ivan Allen took over as mayor. Hartsfield was the perfect choice for Papy's successor. The fair was a Georgia institution, not only renowned for its stock-car racing and the clamor and clang of its raucous midway, but the site of a famed display of agricultural products, ranging from livestock and poultry to rabbits and roses, from Shetland ponies to talking parrots, from garden clubs to canning clubs, from Boy Scouts to Senior Citizens. Though Hartsfield knew little about livestock, poultry, and home canning, and cared less, the active promotion of the fair in all its facets could keep him in the public spotlight, which he loved. He cared little for sports either. Baseball bored him; he attended wrestling matches only because wrestling promoters paid the city good money for rental of the auditorium. (When his successor, Ivan Allen, announced his plans for a huge new stadium, Hartsfield urged that it be built at Lakewood as part of the Southeastern Fair complex. When this did not happen, he was not greatly perturbed, and thereafter he seemed to take a kind of wry pride in the fact that he would go down in history as the mayor who did not build the stadium.) With his lack of enthusiasm for sports, it was notable that one of his first acts as the new president of the Southeastern Fair was to straighten and widen and smooth out the old Lakewood Park racetrack, a dirt strip known to the racing fraternity as a murderous killer, full of potholes, where to lose control on a curve meant car and driver either went into the wall or into the lake. Hartsfield made a fine new track of it, because he knew the strong hold that dirt-track racing, with its traditional aura of good ole boys running mountain liquor out of the hills, had on thousands of Georgians.

For his first year out of office—in fact for most of the years thereafter—Hartsfield, as mayor emeritus, was as much in the public eye as he had been as mayor. As spring came, the elder statesman began, said editor Eugene Patterson, to "sprout political maxims like a spring lawn sprouts wild onions." Hartsfield's aim was to speak in praise of the May primary, as against a December election, but he used Patterson's column as a podium to utter one of his panegyrics about Atlanta:

People go around mad in the winter. They've spent all their money. They're cold. The trees are bare. They can't get holes in the street fixed because you can't pour asphalt in bad weather. It's a wonderful time for the outs to get in.

But in the springtime in Atlanta—ah, . . . What a beautiful town this is. The sun comes down and warms the heart. The trees bud and the flowers bloom. And everybody in this town is happy. How can they be mad with the men in office? Nobody can be mad in Atlanta in the spring. If you want to stay in office, the time to vote is near.[3]

Another triumph of his first spring as a private citizen in a quarter century came in late April, when he stood in a packed federal courtroom, with his friend and fellow lawyer Morris Abram, to hear a young federal judge named Griffin Bell read the death knell of the county-unit system. For Hartsfield and Abram it was the end of a battle that had begun for both of them nearly twenty years before. To Hartsfield, a city man to the core, it meant that the urban areas at last had come into their own. With the city man's vote no longer diluted, the state could draw from the great wells of political talent in the cities. Georgia could now go on to become a great state. The rural areas, he said, need not worry about Atlanta dominating them. "Atlanta," he summed up, "has never been able to agree with itself."[4]

Hartsfield's freedom to take on larger and more varied duties led to an appointment to a Ford Foundation committee for the review and evaluation of the foundation's urban programs. The purpose of the committee, which was made up in large part of professors of sociology and geography, was to discover how well a university could identify and define urban problems— and what the university should do about curing urban ills once they were discovered. The idea seemed to be that the university should turn out individuals trained to function as "urban generalists," who would see the urban picture and see it whole, and out of their special expertise, they could provide political and professional leadership in solving the problems of the cities.

Hartsfield at his first meeting listened to this outline by the committee chairman and was not impressed. To him the universities "have at last discovered a vineyard which the city officials have been planting and pruning for a quarter of a century."[5] He also expressed doubt that a cloistered scholar would be able to identify and put down the type of corruption endemic to city politics. The chairman, James S. Pope, explained to Hartsfield that the idea was that the university should serve as the training ground for the specialists in government; it would not, as Hartsfield seemed to fear, take over quasi-governmental functions. Hartsfield was dubious. "You are going too far. The concept of training is sound. If you are going to do what the city should be doing, that is wrong."

The discussion turned to the slums—with some of the more cloistered deans suggesting that the slum problem should be attacked first by "arousing the pride of the people." Hartsfield's

Three men who changed Atlanta. Robert Woodruff (left) talks with Bill Hartsfield and Ivan Allen, two mayors he liked and trusted and to whom he gave his full support, 1961.

Photo by Jack Kanel; courtesy of the Woodruff Library, Emory University

Atlanta in 1961, the year Hartsfield stepped down as mayor.

And Hartsfield International Airport, his proudest monument, as it appeared that same year.

Courtesy of the Atlanta Historical Society

Photo by Cary B. Wilmer, Jr.;
courtesy of the Woodruff Library, Emory University

Hartsfield and Tollie, early 1960s.

Courtesy of the Woodruff Library, Emory University

Family portrait. Hartsfield and Tollie, and her son
Carl Tolan, shortly after their marriage in 1962.

answer was a snort. "Some people can't be 'roused; like slum landlords," he said.

Hartsfield, after listening to the learned scholars, came up with his own summary of what he felt should be the relationship between university and urban center. First, every university should have in its library a special collection of manuscripts and statistical studies dealing with urban problems. The university should turn out planners, all right, but planners who could fit plans to the ability of a city to carry them out. There are, he said, "too many planners who make plans, and have no knowledge of other functions or problems of cities."

His fellow committeemen used such scholarly phrases as getting results by the use of "leverage points" or "multiplier effects." Hartsfield, in plain language, said it all boiled down to translating intelligent plans into political action, without the university getting into trouble with governments. In seminars at colleges all over the country—Rutgers, Purdue, Maryland, Delaware, Pittsburgh, the University of California at Berkeley—Hartsfield discussed the idea that the function of the land grant college and agricultural schools, which send county agents, home demonstration agents, and extension service people into rural areas, could be duplicated by the great urban universities in a sort of citified 4-H club arrangement, by which the city youngster would learn skills typical of his environment. Hartsfield, though, felt that the poor city-dweller was different from the poor farmer. He best could be handled by an honest and intelligent city government rather than by a scholar from the university.

"Certain functions of government must be carried out by local government. The theory of federal funds for urban renewal is based on local government taking action . . . I speak out of a wealth of experience, about getting people to act, such as slum landlords." The university, he hinted, in trying to plan for urban renewal could, without being aware of it, put itself in conflict with the local slum landlords. There was, of course, a way by which the slum owners could be put down. Publicity, Hartsfield said, would ruin them.

Hartsfield, for all his doubts about the practical judgment of his fellow committeemen, enjoyed his term of service on the Ford Foundation and easily gained the attention of his more erudite colleagues. The next year another appointment came his way that was also a tribute to his specialized knowledge. He was made a member of the Rockefeller Brothers' Fund, a twenty-five-man panel to investigate and evaluate the condition of the performing arts in America; the panel was to conduct a six-month study to determine how the arts are financed and how much business and government contribute.

For a man proud of his instinct for keeping aware of progressive ideas and practices in all fields having to do with the public weal, from garbage disposal to the arts, Hartsfield had one curious blind spot. He was absolutely and irrevocably opposed to the fluoridation of city water for the protection of the public's teeth; and he would not permit the treatment of Atlanta's water with fluorides as long as he was mayor. Then, and thereafter, he wrote, spoke, and vehemently argued that any city government that fluoridated its water was poisoning its people. This attitude later brought him into brief conflict with his friends at Coca-Cola to whom he was greatly obligated.

When Chip Robert and Hartsfield were wandering the world in the fifties, the Coca-Cola people in foreign lands made smooth their path and opened all doors for them. When in the sixties Hartsfield traveled abroad with his new wife, Tollie, they did the same thing. She recalls one incident when they were touring Europe in 1963. In Brussels they were invited to a reception by the king and queen at the palace. (Mayor Allen had named Hartsfield as his representative to a meeting of the International Union of Local Governments.) Afterward they were to go on to dinner with the Burke Nicholsons, the representatives of Coca-Cola in Brussels. Tollie found herself engaged in animated conversation with Queen Fabiola, with King Baudouin standing by, the queen saying that she would very much like to come to America sometime, and Tollie answering that she would be most welcome in Atlanta. As the talk went on she felt a tug at her elbow and Hartsfield's voice in her ear, a whisper that all standing by could hear, "Come on, Tollie, the Nicholsons are waiting to take us to dinner."

His friendship with the head of Coca-Cola, Robert Woodruff, was deep and enduring. They rode the town together in the evenings, visited back and forth on Sundays, and the Hartsfields frequently called on him on Saturdays after a football game at Tech. On one such visit Tollie was wearing a very large and noticeably fashionable hat. Woodruff looked at it and asked Hartsfield how much the Ford Foundation was paying him for his services as a consultant. Hartsfield said it wasn't the money, it was the prestige—pronouncing it *press*tige, as he always did, Tollie noticed. "You didn't buy that with '*press*tige,'" grinned Woodruff, pointing at the hat.

Hartsfield's pay from the Ford Foundation was a hundred dollars a day for each day he served, and from The Coca-Cola Company he received six thousand dollars (and later three thousand dollars) a year, and he gave each full measure of his time and thought. In 1963 a distinguished firm of Atlanta architects, Edwards and Portman, came up with the idea of a huge civic and cultural center to be constructed in the heart of downtown, to be known as Coca-Cola Center. The building, which would take over several blocks now partly occupied by the Regency Hotel, would house the national headquarters of Coca-Cola, as well as providing a complex of theaters, auditoriums, symphony halls, and space for commercial exhibits. The Coca-Cola Company, ever on the lookout for ways to serve the community which would enhance its own image as a good citizen, was willing to consider the proposal—until they asked Harts-field for his advice. He told them bluntly to forget it. The city would have title to the complex, but popular subscription would be required to raise the funds to build it, a situation that would give people the idea that they were being asked to con-tribute to The Coca-Cola Company. "From the standpoint of the Company," he wrote, "I would not recommend this sug-gested wedding of the Company, with its prestige, and Atlanta's cultural need."[6]

Hartsfield, however, was in thorough agreement that Atlanta needed such a center, embracing a concert hall seating at least twenty-five hundred people, where plays, concerts, and lectures might be held, with adequate space for scenery storage and rehearsal halls, and a small theater for local schools and col-leges and little theater groups. Architect Henry Toombs, he pointed out, had designed such a complex for Piedmont Park near the Twelfth Street entrance, and this, in Hartsfield's view, came nearer to filling the real needs of the town than any other plan that had been suggested.

The Coca-Cola Center downtown did not come to pass, nor did the center in Piedmont Park, when a bond issue to build it failed. But Hartsfield's deep commitment to the arts profoundly interested his friend Woodruff, and with his strong support much that Hartsfield thought was needed was created. The Memorial Arts Center was built four years later—with the firms of Toombs, Amisano and Wells, and Stevens and Wilkinson de-signing the complex of theaters that Hartsfield had envisioned. The huge auditorium he had recommended came into being the next year, with construction of the Civic Center as a home for the biggest commercial exhibits and the setting for Atlanta's greatest cultural event—the annual visit by the Metropolitan Opera.

At the same time he was urging the construction of a civic and cultural center, he was strongly opposing a plan by the

General Services Administration to bring twenty-five federal agencies and the United States District Court together in one huge building in downtown Atlanta. His reasons were simple: federal buildings paid no city taxes, not even a sanitary tax, and there was a surplus of office space in the city already. "Atlanta needs this like it needs a hole in the head," he told the papers.[7]

He also came out swinging and bellowing "NO" when a proposal was made to change the name of Decatur Street to "East Marietta," joining Atlanta historian Franklin Garrett in a successful drive to kill the measure.

Obviously Hartsfield in his retirement was as busy as ever he was as mayor and involved in many of the same projects that had interested him over the years. He bitterly, and successfully, opposed the creation of a second passenger airport in Henry County because it would be nearer to Macon than to Atlanta, and his profound interest in garbage paid off in honors when in May 1963 a new incinerator was named for him—a fitting tribute, according to editor Eugene Patterson. "After all what more appropriate monument could be raised to the hottest-tempered old tyrant in the municipal annals of benevolent despotism than a roaring, 1,500-ton fountain of blue blazes," wrote Patterson. "Where is the man who has done more slow burns, roasted more enemies alive, thrown up more smoke screens or carried more coals to Newcastle than the former mayor who will be honored by a city that was shaped brick by brick in the kiln of his irascible genius? Bill Hartsfield never cooled off in twenty-three years as mayor. Now his temperature belongs to the ages."[8]

Hartsfield's sardonic wit stayed with him, and his comments on his own condition and on politics in general remained as acerbic as ever. When asked if he missed being mayor he said, yes, he missed the free car and gas the city had provided for him. When the city erected steel barriers in a racially troubled neighborhood in an effort to stop black families from moving into an all-white neighborhood, Hartsfield dashed off an observation that proved as enduring as his whole-horse-in-the-office quip. "Ivan," he said, speaking of his friend Mayor Allen and the fence that had caused a civic uproar, "should learn never to make a mistake they can take a picture of."[9]

Keeping Atlanta as a city with a white majority still obsessed him, and he spoke out incessantly for the annexation of Sandy Springs, North Atlanta, and Druid Hills. As mayor he had had to deal somewhat indirectly with the fact that the flight of the affluent educated white residents to the suburbs was leaving a black central city. As mayor emeritus he could, and did, speak out more forcefully with less care that he not wound the feelings of the blacks or lose their vote. Speaking before the North DeKalb Rotary Club, he said bluntly that if the exodus of moneyed whites to the suburbs continued, the central city would come under Negro domination, a situation which would be bad for the Negro himself. "What good will it do the Negro citizen to go off and leave the town to him. The worst element of his own race will rise up and take over."[10]

He had been even more vehement in an earlier speech before Sigma Delta Chi, the national professional journalistic fraternity. Inspired by sit-ins and demonstrations that were going on in Atlanta at the moment, he said that the Negro community was producing its own rabble-rousers—just as the white communities had in the past—and now the better individual in the black community was afraid to speak out for fear of being called an "Uncle Tom."

Hartsfield was in New York when the rowdiest of the sit-ins took place at Leb's Restaurant in Atlanta, and at first he was horrified. Then he realized that the rebellious blacks were being hauled off by black policemen, and the city officials remained calm, making no rash or intemperate statements. This made him proud of the town. The blacks, he indicated, hurt their own cause by their behavior at Leb's.

He also had some kind words to say about the way his successor, Ivan Allen, was handling the sit-in situation. (Allen, in this instance, had shown great courage in going into the midst of a howling black mob and was saved from injury only by the intervention of his police chief Herbert Jenkins.) Allen, Harts-field said, realized what a lot of Atlanta merchants still did not realize—"that we can't run this great metropolitan city under a set of rules different from those in Kansas City or New York or any other place. The hotel and restaurant people ought to learn the facts of life. The sooner we do it, desegregate and forget it, the better."[11]

This represented a considerable change in Hartsfield's own thinking. Jake Carlton and other Atlanta journalists who had transferred to Washington recall that Hartsfield, when visiting them years earlier, would sometimes embarrass them by his audible comments when he found himself sitting next to black diners in a Washington restaurant.

Hartsfield, as the years passed, grew more and more inclined to reminisce, and reporters found him as quick with a colorful comment as they always had. Nearly any big event could trig-ger his memory. The day President Kennedy was killed in Dallas he came to the *Journal* city room to keep up with the breaking news. There he spoke to Raleigh Bryans of his own fears of assassination. Any public official who takes a strong stand on controversial matters should have a genuine concern for his own personal safety, he said. For the first time he re-vealed publicly, without being dramatic about it, that for many years he had felt that what did happen to Kennedy might at any time have happened to him.

"For the last fifteen years I was in office, after I knew the race issue was emotional, I formed the habit of watching everybody in front of me and in back of me."[12] He kept his car in good working order, fearing a breakdown in some isolated spot, and in the glove compartment he always carried a tear-gas gun and a loaded pistol. When driving alone around town at night, he would immediately head for the first lighted area and turn around if he thought a car was following him.

He had reason to be concerned. Klansmen and other racists have long memories, and even after he had left the mayor's office, the harassment continued. Anonymous callers would phone the house and ask to speak to "that nigger lover," Tollie Hartsfield recalls. Mrs. Mattie Deadwyler, their black cook, unperturbed, would hand the phone to Hartsfield, saying without expression, "It's for you."

Most of his memories, however, were pleasant ones. One vivid one was of the day in 1962 when frock-coated Attorney General Robert Kennedy presented him to practice before the Supreme Court in the last days of the county-unit fight, a day that marked Kennedy's first and Hartsfield's only appearance before that court. The visit of President Lyndon B. Johnson to Atlanta in May 1964 set him off on a long reminiscence of other presidential visits, going back to Theodore Roosevelt, who came to Atlanta in 1906. Hartsfield remembered the parade that escorted him down Peachtree. President William Howard Taft came to eat barbecued possum at a Chamber of Commerce dinner at the city auditorium in 1909, and Taft Hall there was named for him, possibly in apology for feeding him possum. Hartsfield's memories of F.D.R.'s visits were particularly vivid, for he was himself in public life by then, and when Roosevelt's train, en route to Warm Springs, Georgia, stopped at Terminal Station, Hartsfield would go down to visit with him for fifteen minutes. Roosevelt, Hartsfield remembered, would start talking as soon as Hartsfield entered the "Ferdinand Magellan," the president's private car, and would talk without ceasing until the train bumped and Marvin McIntyre told Hartsfield it was time to leave. Roosevelt was perhaps the only man with whom Hartsfield was never able to get a word in edgewise. In a symbolic sense, though, Hartsfield did have the last word. On the morning Roosevelt died at the Little White House at Warm

Springs, Hartsfield had a huge "City of Atlanta" wreath made up. As the train bearing Roosevelt's body came into the Terminal Station, Hartsfield went aboard carrying the wreath, shook hands with Mrs. Roosevelt, expressed the sorrow he and other Atlantans felt, and placed the wreath in the car with the casket.

Going against his long-held belief that no man should allow any statue to be erected in his honor during his lifetime, Hartsfield in early 1964 sat for a portrait bust by Atlanta's nationally famed sculptor, Julian H. Harris. Commissioned by some fifty of Hartsfield's old friends, the bust was unveiled at the Capital City Club, with Tollie Hartsfield making a gracious speech. Harris said later that no portrait bust he had ever done had more deeply involved his own feelings about his subject than this one had. He had known Hartsfield for years; the mayor had commissioned him to do the then avant-garde mobile at the airport, a melody of dangling colored metal shapes, and when the piece aroused wide controversy, Hartsfield had stoutly defended both the work and the artist. Also he indirectly elicited from a viewer a comment that poignantly brought into focus what Harris had been trying to do in creating this work. Hartsfield brought a little blind girl to Harris's studio to "see" the quarter-scale model of the mobile with the sensitive fingertips that served as her eyes. For a long moment she ran her fingers over the gently moving forms. Then she said, "It looks just like a musical instrument sounds." To both Harris and Hartsfield it was the perfect comment. Five years later, when a new row arose over the use of advertising displays in the airport terminal, Hartsfield recalled the famous controversy over the mobile's value as a work of art and gave voice to his own strongly held views on the partnership between fine art and big business.

When we were completing the new airport terminal, we asked Julian Harris to come up with some sort of art, making use of the seal of the city. Other cities had big world maps and globes in their terminals, but we wanted something distinctive of Atlanta.

About that time Alexander Calder had installed a controversial mobile in a New York terminal. Mr. Harris came up with his now famous mobile, depicting Atlanta in the jet age, the seal with tongues of flame and projecting spears.

We knew it would be controversial. That's what we wanted. That mobile literally made the press of the nation. It was better than the story we invented about a pigeon flying into the front door of the Cyclorama and lighting on one of the trees.

The price was $35,000. This scared me a little, but chairman Jesse Draper and manager Jack Gray stood by me, and the work was commissioned. Pictures were carried all over the country, incidentally describing the terminal; letters went to the press, and it even got denounced from a pulpit. We got ten times the cost in free publicity.

And now it is still at work generating more stories. Maybe we could have a new fight about it every five years.[13]

The year brought honors other than having his features immortalized in bronze by sculptor Harris. Oglethorpe University gave him an honorary degree. Lyndon Johnson, knowing that his highly controversial civil-rights bill was going to run into fierce opposition in the South, called on Hartsfield as a private citizen to use his influence to promote a spirit of acceptance and the observance of the law in his own community. In a long telegram he urged Hartsfield to serve on a "committee of distinguished citizens from all walks of life" who would assist communities in providing equal treatment and opportunity for all Americans by "preventing or resolving racial disputes and tensions through reason, persuasion and conciliation." Hartsfield wrote back the same day, saying, "As one who had pioneered for many years in this field, I will be glad to be of any service."[14]

Hartsfield's genius for publicity manifested itself in his handling of the Southeastern Fair. One of the spectacular shows there was a fireworks display depicting the burning of Atlanta. To be sure that the town was aware of the show, he brought to Atlanta from Pennsylvania a great-great-grandson of General

W. T. Sherman, a young steel-company executive named William Tecumseh Sherman Fitch. The story got good play in the papers, but the display that the general's descendant watched was a fizzle. Rain had dampened the fuses.

One small mishap as the year drew to a close gave the city a chuckle at Hartsfield's expense. He got lost on his way to the airport. When he turned off the expressway onto the brand-new connector that he himself had strongly sponsored, he felt highly pleased that at last he and thousands of others could get from downtown to the airport without creeping through the stoplights along the two-lane streets in Hapeville. But he missed the exit ramp to the airport—Hartsfield never did pay much attention to where he was going in an automobile—and was moving rapidly through south Clayton County before he discovered his mistake.

Hartsfield was a fantastically stubborn man, and he continued to sound off, loud and clear, on two subjects close to his heart—the Chattahoochee River and fluoridation. A letter from Caughey Culpepper, general manager of the Atlanta Freight Bureau, urged Hartsfield to lay aside for a moment his suspicions of the motives of anybody living on the Chattahoochee south of Atlanta and join with them in forming the Greater Chattahoochee Development Association. The purpose of this organization would be to convince the citizens of Columbus that they should no longer selfishly block the cutting of a barge channel all the way to Atlanta. Columbus, Culpepper pointed out, could never generate enough barge traffic alone to become a port city. But navigation to Columbus would be made profitable if it were on a longer route, starting in Atlanta and passing through Columbus, to and from the sea. "Such an organization would be doubly effective if it had your support," Culpepper wrote Hartsfield, "and might not even get off the ground without your backing."[15]

Hartsfield wrote back that he would work heartily with any-

one, "provided their goal was the same as his—to make the
Chattahoochee navigable to Atlanta as soon as possible."[16]

The Chattahoochee development never came off, of course;
nor was Hartsfield successful in another field which also had
become an obsession with him—the prevention of the fluoridation of Atlanta water. He wrote to health scientists all over the
world, asking their opinion of the effect on the human body of
the long-term ingestion of fluorides, and he wrote to magazine
editors who had published articles on the subject, damning
those who approved fluoridation, praising those who had opposed it. As his interest in minerals had given him the knowledge and the vocabulary of a trained geologist, he could speak
with equal fluency of the chemistry of the fluoride ion and its
behavior in hard or soft waters or in human bodies of different
ages and metabolisms. He had been converted from an acceptance of fluoridation to a fanatic antagonism by Dr. Alton Oschner, a New Orleans surgeon, who gave him scientific arguments
that changed his mind completely. (Dr. Oschner's article on the
evils of smoking also scared him so badly he gave up cigars.)

His harshest language was reserved for the American Dental
Association and the United States Public Health Service. The
Dental Association, he said, advised local groups to attack
anybody who opposed fluoridation as "crackpots, Ku-Kluxers,
Birchites, or anti-Semites—whichever might have the most political value in that part of the country."[17] The USPHS earned an
even more severe denunciation from Hartsfield. Its motive, he
said, was not only to prevent cavities "but to establish the
precedent of medicating water and bridging the gap between
the power of government to medicate for non-communicable
diseases."[18] In general, Hartsfield, when he got worked up, was
as vicious in his denunciation as he accused the American Dental Association of being. To him they were "fanatic zealots,"
"welfare zealots" who were suggesting that other medicated

chemicals be put in water supplies. To Hartsfield this was mad-
ness, and once started there would be no end to it.[19]

Early in 1965 Hartsfield heard about a study that excited
him greatly. Conducted by Western Electric, it indicated that
by the year 2000 Atlanta would be among the four major cities
of the nation. He found this forecast very easy to believe, he
told Pollard Turman, president of the Atlanta Chamber of
Commerce, in a letter which he also sent to Robert W. Woodruff, James D. Robinson, Mills B. Lane, Mayor Ivan Allen, Jr.,
Jack Tarver, Opie Shelton, and John Sibley. The only thing that
might interfere with this great achievement, he added, returning to an old and favorite theme, "will be our failure to follow
racial trends and insure good government inside corporate Atlanta by annexation of Sandy Springs, North Atlanta, and Druid
Hills, so as to preserve the proper white balance which is so
necessary for amicable relations between both races." Atlanta,
Hartsfield went on, was saved by the Plan of Improvement in
1952, and "we must do it again or imperil the future control of
over $700,000,000 in magnificent municipal facilities." "The
leading citizens of our town," Hartsfield argued, "should get
together, using the Chamber of Commerce as a banner to be
waved aloft, for immediate study and action. It will take the
best efforts of the power structure to convince the leading officials of Fulton and DeKalb that this must be done for the larger
interests of the area as a whole." He suggested that twenty-five
leading Atlanta citizens get together in a private session to lay
plans for the annexation campaign. Otherwise, he indicated,
within five or six years Atlanta would be 50 percent black,
"with further racial imbalance, toward the black side, going
ahead at an accelerated pace."[20]

If Hartsfield's deeply held fear of a black-dominated Atlanta
ever reached the ears of Martin Luther King, Jr., or Ralph
Abernathy and Andrew Young, King's associates in the South-

ern Christian Leadership Conference, they gave no sign of dis-approval. In a warmly expressed and seemingly sincere letter, King wrote to the mayor emeritus thanking him for joining with other prominent Atlantans in sponsoring his Nobel Prize dinner.

> I must confess that few events have warmed my heart as did this occasion. It was a testimonial not only to me but to the greatness of the City of Atlanta, the South, the nation and its ability to rise above the conflict of former generations and really experience that beloved community where all differences are reconciled and all hearts in harmony with the principles of our great Democracy and the tenets of our Judeo-Christian heritage.

In a handwritten postscript, he added, "I will never forget the great role you played. Your life and dedicated leadership have been great inspirations to all of us."[21]

Two weeks later the Reverend Mr. King might have been somewhat less pleased with Hartsfield's views. Dedicated to nonviolence, King had urged the nation to boycott Alabama products in the drive for voting rights in that state. Hartsfield, speaking at a Brandeis University seminar on violence, said that trying to boycott Alabama would be like trying to "boycott a square yard of water in a lake." A boycott of a state whose economy could not be separated from that of the nation could not be intelligently applied. As for civil-rights violence, he said it was a national problem, as prevalent in the North as in the South. "It is just more magnified in the South," he told his Yankee audience.[22]

Hartsfield's idea that the inner-city racial balance should be maintained at a white majority was predicated on his conviction that the Negro living in a community controlled by the upper-class white would be far better off than he would be living in a fifty-fifty or a black-controlled city, where both races would probably be dominated by the worst elements of each. He made this point often to the black community—and they seemed to listen. And not only the black leaders but the ordinary good folk among them expressed their gratitude and poured out their hopes and fears to him. One correspondent, M. M. Melson, wrote a touching letter, describing how Atlanta's Negroes—hard-working couples, most of them in domestic service—had wanted to live in clean new houses of their own instead of paying fifty dollars a month rent for half of a dilapidated house that had been abandoned by white tenants. But when the FHA built good new houses for them, at a price they could afford, transportation across town by Gray Lines Bus and Atlanta Transit cost them seventy-four cents a day, which was more than they could afford to pay. Nor could their elderly, sick, or poor employers afford to carry the burden for them. Melson said he had asked one high official what the Negro should do about this problem and got the calm answer that they should leave their new houses and move back down to Five Points. Melson concluded by telling Hartsfield, "I have more confidence in your suggesting to the proper authorities a solution of this difficult problem, than I have in anyone else's doing it."[23]

The fear of the Negro as a neighbor had many facets, some even affecting the future of the city as a center of music and the arts. In Ivan Allen's first year a bond issue to build a great cultural center in Piedmont Park had failed when northside realtors spread the word that this would bring on an incursion of blacks into the all-white northside. Now a campaign to raise money by popular subscription to place the center on Peachtree Street, in the same block with the old High Museum and School of Art, was having heavy going. A committee of distinguished Atlantans working hard to raise funds was making some progress, but in Hartsfield's view the project had too many voices.

"My own experience as Mayor," he wrote to his friend Robert Woodruff, "taught me that big names in the community, loaded down with honors, make poor supervisors. They are always attending to other affairs, out of town, etc." Hartsfield's suggested solution was, one, to name a first-class, hard-nosed, practical manager to represent the loose "big shot" committees in daily contacts with architects and builders. Next, he said, he would drop the word "culture." Instead, Hartsfield suggested, "Let your friends start a movement to call it the Woodruff Center. New York has a Lincoln Center. Why not a similar name for Atlanta? This great center . . . will exist for hundreds of years after you are gone, and you cannot be remembered as Mr. Anonymous." "As I see it," he concluded, "there are but two choices—either abject failure or your rescuing the center project, and making it truly one of the great benefactions of the nation." [24]

Woodruff's modesty was genuine. He wanted no great arts alliance named for him (it was eventually named instead in memory of the Atlanta cultural leaders who died in the crash of a chartered plane at Orly Airport, Paris, in 1962), but behind the veil of anonymity Woodruff did rescue the operation and send it on its way to a soundly financed and influential future. In what could truly be called "one of the great benefactions of the nation," he gave some nine million dollars to the building fund, and endowments bringing the total gift to nearly twenty-five million dollars.

Hartsfield throughout the year was for one reason or another at war with state and federal highway officials. A new perimeter expressway, to be called Interstate 485, was proposed by these agencies, and Hartsfield, in a towering rage, opposed it on the grounds that it would "demolish the beautiful Morningside section adjacent to Piedmont Road." It was, he felt, a monstrosity that public sentiment should immediately condemn since it would literally destroy one of corporate Atlanta's last remaining residential areas. He put all these thoughts on a handbill entitled "Warning, the Bulldozers are Coming," which was sent to Morningside residents over the name of Mr. and Mrs. George R. Newton, Hartsfield's old neighbors on Pelham Road. Despite all protests, a route was surveyed and houses along its right-of-way were bought, but ten years later the houses were still standing, falling into decay. The bulldozers had not come; the road had not been built.

In mid-June 1966 word from California that David O. Selznick had died set Hartsfield off on a flood of reminiscences about one of the great events of his life—the *Gone with the Wind* premiere in 1939. A year later the death of Vivian Leigh, who had played Scarlett in the movie, loosed another tide of memories. He remembered riding with Miss Leigh from the airport to the Georgian Terrace Hotel along a parade route lined with three hundred thousand people, a blissful moment for the beaming mayor. In 1961 she and Selznick were both in Atlanta again for a second premiere of the picture. As he met her he swept off his hat, bowed, and said gallantly, "Time has dealt lightly with our Scarlett." It served perhaps to soothe Miss Leigh's feelings, bruised earlier in a New York airport press conference when a young reporter asked her what role she had played in *Gone with the Wind*.[25]

Hartsfield's fondness for recalling the days gone by while showing an amazingly varied and imaginative interest in the future was evident on state primary election night in Atlanta, September 14, 1966. The old election-night sport of campaign-headquarters-crawling was not what it used to be, he told Celestine Sibley of the *Constitution*. Everything had become mechanized. Computers were predicting results, and the candidate who in the old days would be issuing victory statements all night, now was gloomily, or cheerfully, watching television as his fortunes ebbed or soared. Hartsfield was making his observation in the headquarters of his favorite, Ellis Arnall, whose headquarters Miss Sibley said most nearly resembled the crowded, noisy, merry, smoke-filled bailiwick of old. Headquarters of the other candidates—Lester Maddox and James Gray—tended to be on the dull side, though in their suite at the Dinkler, Jimmy Carter and Rosalynn and their three children were cheerful enough. The television reports showed Carter running in second place.[26]

If the primary bored him, events leading up to the general election set Hartsfield, the old political war-horse, to shaking his mane tentatively, stomping the ground a little, and sniffing the battle afar off. In short, when Charles Weltner shocked and confused Fulton County Democrats by withdrawing from the Fifth District congressional race, claiming he could not sign the pledge to support Lester Maddox, the party's candidate for governor, the desperate Democrats cast about for a candidate to oppose Republican Fletcher Thompson. Hartsfield's name was high on the list of those first mentioned. His reaction: "Like all citizens I am doing some soul-searching as to what is best for our beloved state and city. I am sorry Charles Weltner has withdrawn but I understand his high principles which he puts above public office, and pay tribute to this Georgia profile in courage." The Fifth District needed experience and competent service in Washington more than ever, Hartsfield continued, adding, "I have not been a seeker after any office save that which the people honored me for nearly twenty-five years. However, I must confess that this unexpected situation has me thinking more seriously as to what is best for us all." Then, when a reporter asked him if he would accept the nomination if it were offered to him, he said, "If they felt I was the best man and that I could be of service, I would be most seriously inclined to accept."[27]

Hartsfield's love for his city was known and recognized. His professed love for the state and for the counties around Atlanta was a new thing, for he had always gone on the assumption that his beloved city was encircled by a ring of rural enemies. Democratic politicians on the state and county level were aware of his attitude, and Hartsfield was not called upon to make the sacrifice, at age seventy-six, of pulling up stakes and moving to Washington.

The year, though, was not without its honors. On the night of October 16 his friend and longtime supporter Abe Goldstein, former national commissioner of B'nai B'rith, personally presented him with the first Abe Goldstein Human Relations Award of the Anti-defamation League of B'nai B'rith. The award was for the "dignity" with which he had handled the city's offices for so many years. But in his acceptance speech he returned to his ancient angry theme. Atlanta was an island of wisdom, virtue, and progress, surrounded by a hostile county-unit state.

THE CURTAIN FALLS

THOUGH HARTSFIELD in his retirement from politics went back intermittently to his original profession, the practice of law (which meant, mainly, trying to help his friends with their local tax problems), his overwhelming interest was not the law but his job as director of the Southeastern Fair Association. Every day the year round he spent at least a few hours at Lakewood Park, and during the fair season he was there from early morning to late at night. On the grounds he scurried about in an electric golf cart, a menace to pedestrians. When feeling the need for a broader look he would take a helicopter ride over the fairgrounds and the surrounding area, complaining bitterly that expressway construction adjacent to Lakewood was not going fast enough.

He reached new heights of eloquence with his description of the sights and sounds and smells of the fair. The "mooing cattle, grunting hogs, [the sight] of chickens and rabbits, of balloons, cotton candy, hot dogs, flower shows, home-cooked pies, Senior Citizens and contests, Army, Navy, Air Force exhibitions, beauty contests, school bands, church booths, merry-go-rounds, square dancing, side show barkers, and then the fireworks—all are part of it." Hartsfield uttered this litany of praise at a hearing in Washington, D.C. before a Senate committee on patents, trademarks, and copyrights. All these good things, he said, were meaningless if they were not seen, heard, smelled, and savored against a background of music. What was concerning him was a proposed new copyright bill that would impose heavy penalties on organizations playing recorded music without getting permission or paying a fee. Fairs, he argued, which were "part of the folkways of America, contributing to the pleasure of little children and the education and entertainment of young and old," should be exempt from such an impost, as should any civic event "sponsored by states, counties, municipal governments or non-profit civic clubs."[1]

Another attempt by government to regulate the lives of his fellow Georgians to what he believed to be their detriment led to another vicious forensic battle—which Hartsfield lost. A new federal act would put all the United States on daylight saving time from April through October. This in Hartsfield's view would throw the lives of nearly everybody out of kilter. Georgia in 1941 had reluctantly accepted its place in the eastern time zone, oriented to the New York business day, though 85 percent of the state lay in the longitude of Chicago, which was in the central time zone. To go on daylight saving time, then, would have the effect of imposing a two-hour advance of time in western Georgia. Fortunately the proposed act provided that a state could, by act of legislature, retain its existing time, and Hartsfield was eloquent in his urging that Georgia's legislature defy the federal edict. If not, he argued:

In the hot months of July and August you would lose an hour's restful morning sleep. Little children would go to bed at nine, with the hot sun *still* shining, and the sights and sounds of daylight all around. They would go to school in September and October, *in the dark*. Farmers and laborers would be forced to get up and wait an hour before getting enough light to work. Amusements and evening church services would be disrupted. Thousands of workers living long distances from their jobs would virtually get up in the middle of the night to get to their work on time.[2]

Hartsfield was ever one to peer into woodpiles to see what

dark forces might be lurking there, and in this case he detected several. This effort to force the whole eastern seaboard onto New York daylight saving time was motivated by the big auto-mated computer-operated corporations, and the airlines and network broadcasts, he said, for it would simplify their opera-tions. To Hartsfield with his Southeastern Fair, which needed early darkness for his evening fireworks displays, and to his friend John Stembler, president of a theater chain with many drive-in movies, the equivalent of double daylight saving time would be a disaster. Before it got dark enough for these enter-tainment agencies to function at their best, it would be well past nearly everybody's bedtime. Stembler sent out over his own signature, to congressmen, editors, and government offi-cials, letters prepared by Hartsfield arguing these points with eloquence, but to no avail. Georgia went on daylight saving time.

His interest in protecting and expanding Lakewood Park led him in directions other than his attempt to block legislation he thought would be to its disadvantage. In 1967 he dug up the old red clay strip that was the Lakewood racetrack, widened it by fifteen feet, banked the curves, and laid a new surface smoothed by chloride and water. Then, with the promise that in the following year it would be paved, he brought back NASCAR racing, the stock cars beloved by Georgians. Included in the face lift that restored the old racing strip to use after eight years was a new press box, designed by Hartsfield. An in-dication of his own interest was the fact that he had plenty of space for camera crews and no place where the writing press could put their typewriters. The writers were mildly annoyed by this, for as Hartsfield showed them around the new layout—including driving them around the track in his own car—into the porches of their ears he poured his memories of racing, both on the ground and in the air. He recollected the time he, as a young alderman obsessed with the idea of air travel, put on an air show at the old Candler racetrack; he had six thousand dollars invested in the show, with barnstormer Doug Davis as his feature attraction, but it was actually a dog that saved his investment. He advertised that the dog would be dropped from a plane by parachute. The Society for the Prevention of Cruelty to Animals attacked Hartsfield; the story moved from page ten to page one, and a great throng showed up to see if Hartsfield would defy the dog lovers. He did. The dog was dropped and floated safely down to earth. Later Hartsfield tried dropping a monkey, but it didn't work. "The monkey climbed the shrouds," said Hartsfield, "and had to be pulled back into the plane."[3]

Hartsfield recalled a Labor Day race at Lakewood in 1942, when he was mayor, which was also threatened with disaster, when thirty-eight thousand angry race fans thought for a while that they were not going to see their top favorites race. Some of the best race drivers of the day were liquor runners, and three of the top drivers in the race had been caught at one time or another. But just before the race started there was an announce-ment on the radio saying that the three drivers could not com-pete, for there was a city ordinance prohibiting criminals from driving at Lakewood. "Well, the police said they wouldn't race, and the crowd, 38,000 of them mind you, said they would. Her-bert Jenkins's police held up the start . . . but by this time the crowd was getting mighty unruly, and Jenkins and his boys, they had to choose between a riot and a race. The race won."[4]

As in the old days, when Hartsfield wanted to get something in the paper, he did not send a public relations man; he went himself. One morning he showed up in the *Constitution* city room to announce that he had just booked a hog act for the fair which included pigs singing, sliding down sliding boards, and pushing baby carriages. The hog act's manager, said the mayor emeritus, often took his troop of porkers to civic-club lun-cheons, where they were more happily received than most civic-club speakers.

With Tollie and Carl in tow, Hartsfield traveled across the United States, looking for acts or amusement devices he might import for the fair. In Washington, D.C., after his stint before the senate committee to denounce the copyright act, he spent several days relaxing at the zoo and the Smithsonian. He went to Syracuse, New York, to inspect a merry-go-round, and in St. Louis, Missouri, he was given a personal tour of the zoo by Marlon Perkins, the famed animal authority.

With their friends, architect Henry D. Norris and his artist wife, Hartsfield and Tollie went to Expo 67 in Montreal, where for three days they were housed in "The Habitat," an avant-garde structure that Norris and his wife, as designers and decorators of homes, found exciting. Tollie, being of practical bent, spent her time buying the hardware for a new room that Norris was designing for the Hartsfield home on Stovall Boulevard. It was to have a cathedral ceiling and an unusual fireplace designed by the late architect Henry Toombs. Its purpose was to house and display the hundreds of objects collected by Hartsfield over his years as mayor. These included a merry-go-round horse, carved of wood in Germany, and mementoes of the notables Hartsfield had welcomed to Atlanta—including Charles A. Lindbergh, presidents Roosevelt, Truman, and Kennedy, General Eisenhower when he was supreme commander in Europe, and Madame Chiang Kai-Shek. Pictures of which Hartsfield was particularly proud showed him with David Ben Gurion of Israel, Pope Pius XII, Margaret Mitchell, and the stars of *Gone with the Wind*.

The *Gone with the Wind* pictures were particularly meaningful to Hartsfield, and as 1968 began he was writing to Kay Brown, the artist agent, in New York, "just to renew an old acquaintanceship and to let you know that I am still hitting on all eight cylinders," but actually to find out who, if anybody, had the stage rights to *Gone with the Wind*. As long as he lived Hartsfield was interested in seeing Margaret Mitchell's epic revived—as a stage play, a musical, or whatever. It was said of him that he was one Atlantan who taught his fellow citizens to quit living in the dear dead days of "Before the War" and to turn their faces to the future. And this was true, but it did not apply to his nostalgic memories of 1939, when the spotlight shone on him with Peggy Mitchell, Gable and Leigh, and the star-spangled cast of *Gone with the Wind.*

Hartsfield was sentimental about other matters, too, notably the birthdays of his friends and other eventful dates in their lives. For years, until banker Robert Strickland died, he and Strickland and Ivan Allen, Sr., jointly celebrated their mutual birthday on March 1. In what was to become a pattern over the years, he spent New Year's Eve with realtor John O. Chiles, a man who shared his exuberant faith that each year would be better than the last. He also loved to spend a few days in the fall at Ichauway, as guest of his old friend Bob Woodruff. There he gained reknown by the remarkable feat of shooting at the same turkey five times—once while it was flying toward him, three times while it was sitting in a tree over his head, and once again as it flew away—and missing it each time. He never failed to mark the anniversary date when Woodruff took over at Coca-Cola, for Woodruff became president of the firm in the same year Hartsfield won his first political race, for alderman. His congratulatory note to Woodruff in May 1968 brought a modest and whimsical reply from his friend: "I agree," he wrote, "that Coke and Hartsfield—and the order could be re-versed—have been good for Atlanta but I'm not so sure about the other fellow! Anyway, Coca-Cola, Hartsfield and Woodruff have come along together and done not too badly and I hope that situation will continue to prevail."[5]

Hartsfield's interest in national politics was as keen as ever as the country went into the 1968 election year, but his admiration for the Kennedy family, which centered on the late President John F. Kennedy, did not apply with equal fervor to presidential candidate Robert Kennedy. Hartsfield was a hawk on the Vietnam War, and Kennedy opposed Johnson's Vietnam policy, for which Hartsfield called him the "Bugs Bunny of American politics." He also had sharp criticism of black leaders who, he said, demanded that the United States withdraw from Vietnam so that more money could be spent on problems of the domestic poor. In Hartsfield's words, "To pull out of Vietnam to give the money to the noisy minorities at home would be a course of destruction for the nation."[6]

Hartsfield was as deeply disturbed about political violence born of local differences as he was about those who preached and paraded against violence in Vietnam. In a letter to James Pope, former Atlanta and Louisville, Kentucky journalist, he wrote: "I am one who thinks this country has got to change its whole approach to welfare and crime prevention if we expect to survive as a free nation. We have spent billions on welfare and in coddling racial agitators, only to see the blackened ruins of our principal cities . . . In the meantime Russia is licking us all over the world and particularly in the United States . . . I sincerely hope a wave of conservatism will sweep over us before it is too late."[7]

Another whose conservative views he admired was Vice-President Spiro Agnew. "I congratulate you on your forthright utterances about the phony liberals and so-called intellectuals who have commanded the television scenes for the past few years," he wrote Agnew. "I was Mayor of this city during the days of transition of the South to a more liberal racial policy. I denounced the Ku Klux with all the invective at my command and all the liberals cheered me on."[8]

Hartsfield, who had been privately critical of his successor, Mayor Ivan Allen, for his drive to build a stadium, and who was not entirely convinced that Allen's Model Cities program would work or that a proposed Rapid Transit System—later MARTA—was feasible, had nothing but praise for Allen's handling of the explosive situation existing in Atlanta at the time of the funeral for Martin Luther King, Jr. "I think the whole city, and indeed the entire metropolitan area, owes a debt of gratitude to Mayor Allen, his department heads, his police and fire departments, the Atlanta Transit System, the taxicab companies and others who responded in a time of great stress with a magnificent performance."[9] The eyes of the world were on Atlanta, Hartsfield said, and nothing was done or said in that time to tarnish the name of the city. He was particularly outraged by the violence that had taken place in other cities, notably Newark and Detroit, following King's assassination, a reaction that Senator Herman Talmadge shared.

Hartsfield kept closely in touch with Senator Talmadge on matters having to do with sit-ins, protest marches, and other forms of racial demonstrations, and though Hartsfield had surprised the nation by his calm acceptance of the 1954 school ruling, he and Talmadge held nearly the same views of such institutions as the Southern Christian Leadership Conference. Hartsfield was also sharply critical of certain political actions taken by black leaders such as Representative Grace Hamilton, who in the past he had looked to for advice. In order to broaden the participation of minorities in city affairs, Mrs. Hamilton and representatives Andrew Young and Ben Brown had advocated bills returning the city to ward elections, strengthening the powers of the mayor, and enlarging the city's board of aldermen. Hartsfield appeared before Fulton County legislators to oppose bitterly all these measures. Atlanta had always had city-wide elections until the twenties, but in that decade, he charged, the head of the Ku Klux Klan took over the primary machinery and ordered ward elections. The result, he said, was an era of such "rottenness and corruption" that a grand-jury investigation was held that ended in court trials that sent eight city officials to jail. (The graft probe grew out of the construction of City Hall from 1928 to 1930.) During his four years as

state representative, which followed this turmoil in city government, Hartsfield had helped to abolish ward elections and to
restore city-wide elections; and as mayor emeritus he bitterly
opposed any return to the old graft-ridden system.

Honors came to Hartsfield in 1968, as in years past. Along
with John A. Sibley, Mrs. Bruce Schaefer, and Captain Max Cle-
land, a Vietnam war hero who had lost both legs and an arm in
battle, Hartsfield received a Great Georgian Award, sponsored
by WSB Radio and Atlanta Federal Savings and Loan. Somewhat
more surprising, his old political enemy Governor Lester Maddox asked him to be a delegate to a National Rivers and Harbors Congress to be held in Washington for three days in June.
Their mutual feeling that Georgia should dam her rivers, particularly the Chattahoochee, was perhaps the only subject on
which Hartsfield and Maddox could agree. Unhappily, Maddox noted, there were no funds to cover Hartsfield's expenses
to the convention, which perhaps led Hartsfield to scribble in
pencil on the governor's letter a cryptic "maybe."

Hartsfield, who had spent many hours, days, even years of
time and thought trying to annex to Atlanta adjoining parts of
Fulton County, found himself in 1969 joining in a fight to block
a bill that would legally merge Atlanta and Fulton County. To
the mayor emeritus this meant that his beloved city would
come under the control of those benighted county politicians
whom he had always looked upon as enemies of Atlanta. To
oppose the measure he dug up a law going back to 1945, a so-
called Stop Atlanta measure when it was passed, which pro-
hibited the merger of city and county governments when the
city lay in two counties—as did Atlanta.

Hartsfield, who had basked happily in the limelight when he
received the Abe Goldstein B'nai B'rith medal and the Great
Georgian Award, was equally happy to share the spotlight with
others who deserved recognition. In June 1969, as president of
the Southeastern Fair, he presented to orchestra conductor Al-

bert Coleman a plaque from the Atlanta Federation of Musi-
cians, honoring Coleman on the group's twenty-fifth anniversary. Coleman, who had come to Atlanta to lead the orchestra
at the Roxy Theater during the wartime appearance there of
Abe Marcus's "30 Beautiful Girls 30" stage shows, stayed on
after the war to become famous in Atlanta as organizer and conductor of the Atlanta Pops Orchestra. The orchestra began its
concerts at the Fox Theater, where it was happily received, and
moved from there to Chastain Park when Hartsfield, in the
early fifties, decided that the somewhat bedraggled park should
once again become a cultural center. Hartsfield, who had traveled over the country seeing how other states, North Carolina
particularly, used their open-air amphitheaters, came back to
Atlanta to remodel the park, notably by adding shelters where
people could take cover when it rained.

The free summer concerts at the park for a while were tre-
mendously successful, as they had been at the Fox, where the
Pops had opened in 1944 to an audience of six thousand. "There
was no big league baseball to compete, no color TV . . . the park
was a place to have a good time."[10]

Coleman's musicianship, his ability to discover young talent
and to develop it, kept the Pops in the park going for a while,
but the concerts gradually decreased in number as inflationary
pressures made the city's contribution inadequate. To Hartsfield this was tragic. The people still needed this popular music,
he said, as at the park on July 4 he presented the plaque to
Coleman on the twenty-fifth anniversary of the date when he,
with Hartsfield's blessing, had first presented the Pops in concert.

Though plaques and medals and even a statue or a monument would be acceptable in recognition of a person's civic accomplishments, there were certain other things that Hartsfield
felt should not be bestowed upon any man, no matter how
worthy. He expressed his views bluntly, in a letter to Charlie

Leftwich, who had written him shortly after the death of Ralph McGill. "Dear Charlie," he wrote:

With reference to the suggestion that Plaza Park be renamed for Ralph McGill, if Ralph could speak I do not believe he would want this done.

Plaza Park has long been known as such, and as you know, as Mayor I always opposed renaming streets, parks or public buildings. There is always somebody in the community who wants to take a cheap ride to perpetuate a name by changing a public facility.

Speaking for myself, the only memorial I would appreciate would be that which resulted from the work or money of those who admired me, such as a monument raised by public subscription or some facility where the funds came from those who had respect for me, and not just the cheap renaming of an already existing public facility.

As you know, Ralph McGill was a good friend of mine, and I think the movement of scholarships through his name is just the thing he would appreciate. This, I understand, is being done.[11]

In July 1969 Benjamin E. Mays, president of Morehouse College and one of the distinguished Negro leaders of the century, was writing his autobiography, *Born to Rebel*. In preparing the chapter on Negro-white relations in Atlanta, he wrote to a number of knowledgeable citizens who had lived in Atlanta from thirty years to half a century, asking them to tell him how, and why, did Atlanta, more than any other Southern city, achieve her present good image. To Hartsfield, Mays wrote: "I want to contrast the Atlanta of the late 1960's with what it was in black-white relations in 1921. In the 1920's there wasn't too much difference between Atlanta and Birmingham. Today Atlanta stands among the best cities in the nation in black-white relations. In your opinion, why was it possible for such constructive changes to be made in Atlanta in the past twenty-five years?"[12]

In *Born to Rebel* Mays summarized the varied answers in a paragraph which said that Atlanta, by its climate and location, attracted great numbers of people from other regions, people

who did not have the ingrained prejudices of the native Southerners. But the replies to Dr. Mays's question also placed great
emphasis on municipal leadership, as represented by the three
decades that William B. Hartsfield and Ivan Allen, Jr. served as
mayors of Atlanta. "The leadership of these two men . . . certainly made a colossal difference in bettering human relations
in this city."[13]

Mays's opinion of Hartsfield was to a great extent shaped by
Hartsfield's reaction to an eloquent and moving, but somewhat
inflammatory, "Appeal for Human Rights" prepared by students
of the Atlanta University Center. In clear and forceful language
the students covered all the discrimination, inequalities, and
injustices, in voting rights, jobs, hospitals, housing, restaurants,
theaters, and before the law, which the black had to endure.
And it said specifically that the young generation of blacks
would not wait for the rights which were morally theirs to be
meted out to them one at a time. They ended with the appeal
to all leaders, in government and in civic life, to all ministers
and preachers and men of good will everywhere, to see to it
that these injustices were abolished. The appeal brought strong
protest from many Georgians, who saw it as inspired by communist propagandists. But to Mayor Hartsfield it expressed the
legitimate aspirations of young people throughout the nation
and the entire world. It was, he said, "of greatest importance to
Atlanta."

Though Hartsfield had despised and vigorously opposed the
white element that advocated violence against the Negro and
would deny him the equal rights and opportunities granted to
any citizen, he was equally outspoken in his opposition to
blacks who sought to achieve their own goals by violent means.
In July, on a trip to Europe with Tollie and Carl, he was outspoken in his criticism of black American militants who, he
said, had "destroyed the good image of the Negro" all over

Europe. Europeans, he went on, saw Washington, D.C. "sacked" on television and "wondered if we are going to retain our leadership of the free world."[14]

Hartsfield during 1969 spent much time going through his files, searching for clippings, films, and pictures for wsb television, which was preparing a documentary on the life of Senator Richard B. Russell. Hartsfield himself starred in the documentary, recalling his trips to Washington to see Russell, who was leading the fight for Buford Dam, and offering his suggestion that it should have been named Russell Dam instead. (There was a short-lived movement to name it for Bobby Dodd, the famous Georgia Tech football coach, until somebody pointed out that "Dodd Dam" might be misunderstood when heard on the radio.)

Russell, who always sent Hartsfield warm and friendly greetings at Christmas, expressed his gratitude for Hartsfield's labor on the documentary in a very practical way. The senator persuaded the Grumman Aircraft Company to lend Hartsfield's Southeastern Fair exact replicas of the *Eagle* and *Columbia* spaceships, and NASA sent space suits exactly like those the astronauts had worn in the Apollo moon walk in July. Once assured these items would be on hand, Hartsfield had a replica built of the moon's surface, and Dr. Wernher Von Braun came over from the Space Flight Center in Huntsville, Alabama to cut the ribbon for the project, which showed the *Eagle* on the moon, with its equipment. The wide-eyed audience could hear a tape recording of the astronauts' actual conversation while on the moon's surface.

Hartsfield's showman's instincts told him that there might be those who would not respond to such technical and scientific displays, no matter how incredible they might seem. So he also presented one of the old crowd-pleasers, the Flying Wallendas on the high trapeze—and he opened the fair with the usual parade down Peachtree Street, featuring huge balloons shaped like animals.

On the whole 1969 was a good year. Hartsfield's marriage was going well; he was proud of his beautiful young wife, whose witticisms at dinner parties would send him into gales of laughter; and he had an opportunity, in raising young Carl as his own, to be the kind of father that he had never been able to be to his own son.

One thing that happened did sadden him. In February, Atlanta began to commit what to him still was the crime unthinkable—the fluoridation of the city water supply. Over the years Hartsfield had fought against it, but now, at the last, he fell strangely silent. The reason was simple—he was a pragmatic man; he would fight to the last ditch, but when men to whom he felt deep personal and political obligation—notably his friends at Coca-Cola—began quietly to advise him to devote his crusading zeal to something else, he quickly got the message. By midsummer all the water flowing through Atlanta's taps bore its minute quantity of fluorides. Thus the deed was done, and Hartsfield, though silent, was never reconciled.

Hartsfield was not one to linger long in grieving over lost causes, though. Fluoridation was a fact accomplished, but Ivan Allen, who had brought it to pass, had gone out of office after eight years. Sam Massell was mayor now, and he had announced publicly that in his administration Hartsfield was going to be called on to earn the five hundred dollars a month he drew as mayor emeritus—his function, to guide and counsel the incumbent mayor. (This was a generous, perhaps a placatory, gesture on Massell's part, for in the mayor's race just past, Hartsfield had quietly voted for Rodney Cook, the Republican candidate whom Massell had defeated.)

Hartsfield welcomed the chance to move back into the glare of the political spotlight. In response to Massell's request that he apply his great knowledge of air travel to Atlanta's situation, his first move was to attend a meeting of the aldermanic aviation committee. There he immediately got into a name-calling fight. The controversy was over whether Atlanta should expand its present airport, build a second airport nearby in north Fulton County, or build one in Henry County, south of Atlanta. Hartsfield's view was that if a second airport were built, the Fulton County site would be preferable, but wherever it was to be built, whoever put it there would be hated by those who lived around it. He recalled that many people in Clayton County had put up billboards calling him a thief and a crook and had set off sixteen different investigations seeking to prove their point, including one by the legislature and one by a grand jury, when he started expanding the Atlanta airport in their direction.

As if to prove his point, residents of North Fulton booed Hartsfield loudly when at a public hearing later he again advocated the North Fulton site. And indeed there was reason to suspect that Hartsfield, the incurable city-dweller, did have a faint tinge of malice in his attitude toward the Fulton County site, for the urbanization which always followed airport construction, as it pushed into north Fulton County would invade the quiet retreats of those young and affluent and educated folk who had fled the central city and who had fought all his efforts to annex them in years gone by. Mayor Massell, on his part, wanted the second airport built to the south in Henry County, and Hartsfield's good friend Everett Millican opposed building a second airport anywhere. The best solution, he felt, was to expand the present airport facility. And this, in time, was the decision of the city planning and development committee—thus making possible the great complex which was to become, after his death, a memorial to Bill Hartsfield.

Hartsfield moved into his eightieth year still bright of mind and brisk and brusque of manner, still welcoming the challenge of the future, whether it brought sunshine or stormy weather. Early in the year, a youngster in the eighth grade at Gordon School wrote him a fine round hand, saying that she was preparing a paper on Atlanta and she wanted Hartsfield's opinion on what would be the most pressing problems Atlanta would face in the seventies. Hartsfield was always responsive to the young, particularly the bright ones (he was one of the earliest and strongest supporters of the progressive and permissive Galloway School in Chastain Park), and he answered young Dixie Dowis at some length. "Dear Dixie," he wrote:

Atlanta has a wonderful future which can only be destroyed if the metropolitan area, that is the people in the five counties around it, will [not] allow it to grow and prosper.

If the people insist on moving to the suburbs and then resist the expansion of the city limits, this will finally affect our future government and Atlanta's future will not be bright.

Those who live in the suburbs or small towns around Atlanta are fooling themselves by buying a few years of untroubled existence while the central city goes down. It takes a big city to do big things such as looking after the water supply of millions, big auditoriums, stadiums and airports which only big cities can do.

A city is like a wheel, there is no use depending on good spokes and tires if the hub is rotten. Sooner or later the entire structure will go down.

So, in my opinion, the greatest problem of the 70's is the obligation of the metropolitan area to let Atlanta grow, maintain the racial balance which has made it great and do those things which great cities should do. That is Atlanta's problem of the 70's.[15]

It was his old theme song—the chant that Atlanta was an oasis of industry, education, and culture surrounded by enemies who would do her in. Nor was he any less angry with those he felt would let down America's defenses against her international enemies. In a joint letter to Senator Russell and Senator Talmadge, with copies to the members of the Georgia congressional delegation, he gave his opinion of five senators who had appeared on television to ask that the people write their representatives in Washington demanding that all money to support the Vietnam war be cut off after a certain date. Hartsfield's comments were acid.

Old Ho-Chi-Minh himself could not have done any better than these five traitors. Their naive idea and time limit would amount to a surrender before the world not on the date specified by them but on the date congress passed such a fool law. Their appropriation of funds to repatriate or save our friends left helpless would, of course, be regarded by the North Vietnamese as a hostile act.

Several of these traitors represent fewer people than contained in one ward in Atlanta.

I thank the Lord that our two senators don't have to be implored, but since they invited me to write my views, I think these five men should be accorded the treatment our ancestors gave to Benedict Arnold.[16]

A month later Hartsfield, with Tollie and Carl, was on his way to Hawaii, Japan, Formosa, and Hong Kong to see for himself, close to the point of conflict, what was going on in the Far East.

As usual, when going on a journey, he notified Joe Jones at The Coca-Cola Company of his itinerary, and as usual Coca-Cola people along the way looked out for him. As usual, too, he had his doctor, Mason Lowance, check him over to see that he was fit to make the journey. All seemed well. His heart and lungs were normal, his blood pressure 130 over 90—not bad for a man in his eightieth year.

Despite his good report, however, in the letter of instructions he left for his lawyer, Henry Bowden, there was almost a premonition that time might be running out for him.

Should anything happen to us, this is your authorization to take full charge, both of the office and the house. Tollie has a lot of antiques in the house . . . As to the office, all my duplicate deposit slips and income tax information are on a table in plain view. My will, insurance policies, stock certificates, so forth, are in the false bottom of a small green stool in my dressing room at the house.

I told Charlie Hartsfield [his nephew], he could have a small tin trunk [a gift from his tinsmith father and a treasure since his childhood when it had held his toys], and a hunt board, being family heirlooms, and my motion picture films. I would like for the Historical Society to look around in my den to see if there is anything in the way of mementoes or pictures or clippings which they might want to preserve.[17]

None of these instructions were carried out, of course, for the Hartsfields went through their journey without disaster. Their only moment of concern came when young Carl, exploring Tokyo on his own, was swept up in a passing march of student demonstrators carrying banners. He marched with them awhile and then went back to the hotel carrying a banner. To the dismay of Hartsfield, it bore a slogan denouncing American influence in Japan.

Hartsfield came home to the physical discomfort of a prostate infection that required surgery—and a row over what should be done with Lakewood Park. With his flair for showmanship, Hartsfield had turned the old Southeastern Fair into a highly successful operation, drawing 432,511 customers in 1970, an all-time record. The Fair Association, a subsidiary of the Atlanta Chamber of Commerce, had spent some four million dollars in capital improvements over the years and had offered fifty thousand dollars in prizes and scholarships each year. But there was a growing feeling that not all Hartsfield's talents as a showman could keep the public interested in the educational features and the entertainment the old fair offered. And now at least two million dollars more was needed to take care of two streams running through the property. There was talk at City Hall, therefore, that the three-hundred-acre Lakewood area should be used for other purposes—for low-cost housing, or industrial development, or a park.

To Hartsfield, roaring about the fairgrounds in his three-wheeled scooter, talking to carnival barkers and 4-H club youngsters, and putting pedestrians to flight with his erratic driving, this was outrageous. It was heresy. The fairgrounds, he said bluntly, were for the fair. When the fair closed in early October he immediately began thinking of what he could do to publicize a huge trade show that he was planning to bring there the following May.

He did not live to see that show. Two days before Christmas 1970 he and Tollie attended a wedding at Saint Philip's Cathedral, where the children of two old friends were being married —Jackson Dick's daughter, Jacquelyn, and James Philip Campbell, III. Tollie noticed that as they walked up the hill to the church, the mayor seemed to be panting and gasping for breath. For three days, he told her, he had been a little short of breath. After the wedding, though, he seemed to be feeling better, so they went on to the reception at the Brookhaven Country Club. And there, too, something was different. Usually the mayor was at her side, full of talk and laughter, seeing to it that her champagne glass was never empty, for there was a private joke between them that the more champagne she drank, the more warmly affectionate she became. But this afternoon he was silent, his thoughts seemed far away, and she spent most of her time talking with their old friend Jesse Draper. She noticed that Hartsfield looked drawn and pale, and they went home early.

At the little house on Stovall Boulevard she went in to start supper for him and for her son Carl, and for her father, who was staying with them. They had lived here for nine years, and the little place was already cluttered with memories. Here were the multitude of pictures, certificates, keys to cities, plaques, citations from governors and presidents, tape recordings, movies he had made around the world, all presided over by the carved merry-go-round horse of which he was so proud. There were the little tin trunk his father had made, books galore, and the andirons forged by Alderman Raleigh Drennon. There were the things she had collected—the heartshaped tables with the inlaid lacquer saying "Heartsfields," a play on words reflecting her love for verbal byplay. She remembered that when they bought the house he had had two requirements—that there be only one story, for he hated climbing stairs, and that it be close to Brookhaven Club, so that Carl could walk there to go swimming. One of their early visitors was Robert Woodruff, on a Sunday morning, and she remembered the puzzled look on Woodruff's face when Hartsfield insisted they go out and take a walk. "I want the neighbors to see you," Hartsfield explained. She also remembered the Halloween night when Hartsfield had gone playing trick or treat on neighbor Freeman Strickland—wearing a gorilla suit.

Now there was no more merriment in him. As soon as they got home from the reception he went in and fell across the bed. This she knew was unusual, but she tried to make it seem she was not worried. "What's the matter," she asked, "Did you have too much champagne?" He made the old joke about her heart growing fonder when he plied her with champagne. "I always try to do you in," he said. "Looks like this time I did myself in." He dragged himself to the table, but could not eat. He had, he said, a touch of indigestion.

It was three o'clock in the morning before the pain had gotten so bad he let her call the doctor. Dr. Lowance wasted no words. "Get him to Saint Joseph's," he said. "Now!"

As they laid him on the table in the emergency room at Saint Joseph's, the bad attack came on. His heart stopped beating. Quick action by the staff—using electric shock—got it going again, and slowly, over the next few hours under intensive care, he began to come around. The pain subsided. The wild look went out of his eyes. He could talk, sensibly and calmly, about what had happened and what the future held for him. He did not want the press to know where he was, he said. And for a week there was nothing in the papers or on the air. But the word got out somehow, and on December 30, seven days after he had fallen ill, the *Constitution* had the story—a brief two paragraphs saying merely that Hartsfield was in the coronary unit at Saint Joseph's and was very sick. By afternoon the *Journal* had the full story—of the "massive coronary occlusion" which had left him in "serious" condition.

But the old man was tough. By the next day, December 31, he was sitting up in bed, eating his breakfast. Visitors soon were coming in—first his successors as mayor, Sam Massell and Ivan Allen, then old friends Tommy Reed, Henry Bowden, Robert Woodruff, Abe Goldstein, and Herbert Jenkins. Lyndon Johnson telephoned from the White House. Callers found him bright-eyed, alert, full of curiosity about what was going on in the world outside. "What are they saying about me being sick?" he asked. "They are saying you are too damned stubborn and pig-headed to die," a friend told him. Hartsfield grinned. "That's right," he said.

But he seemed to know, deep down, that the chances were slim indeed that he would live to see his eighty-first birthday, coming up on March 1. He talked calmly to Tollie of his funeral plans. He wanted Graham Jackson to play the accordion at the service, and he wanted it to be held at H. M. Patterson's chapel, a small place, not in the huge sanctuary of the First Baptist Church, where he was a member and where he and Tollie had regularly attended church and Sunday school. The crowd who came to his funeral would be so small, he said, just a few old friends, they would be lost in the big church, and this would be embarrassing. And he wanted the evangelist, the Reverend John Haggai, to say a few words over him.

Even before they were married, realizing the difference in their ages, he had sometimes talked to Tollie about his dying, and he made her promise that when his last hours came she would be there, holding his hand. "They may tell you that I'm unconscious and that I don't know what is going on," he told her. "But you won't know what I'll be conscious of, or what I'll know. So be sure you are holding my hand when I am dying."[18]

And she was. After two months of believing that he was getting better and would soon be all right, she sensed a subtle change in him. The nurses were noncommittal, but when they were out of the room, she peeked at their notes written on his chart. What she saw confirmed her fears. He was dying. And for eighteen hours she stayed with him, holding his hand, and even after his breathing stopped and she knew he was gone, she sat there, head down, still holding his hand. He was conscious to the end, she said, and once, when she felt his feet and found them cold, she made a feeble little jest about his getting cold feet at the thought of going to heaven. He smiled, as he always did when she made a joke. And to the end he kept his own wry humor. Once he began to pray, aloud, and his voice became louder and louder. Tollie, afraid that he would disturb the other patients, told him not to pray so loud—that God could hear him. "I just want to be sure," he said. Again, with a rueful grin he told his doctor, "If I'd known what you were going to do to me, I'd never have gotten in the car."

He died shortly before midnight on the evening of February 22, 1971—two months after the first attack—a week before his birthday. The service was held on February 25 at Spring Hill as he had wished. And as Tollie had predicted, the crowd overflowed the little chapel. Dr. Haggai's remarks in remembrance were brief, simple, and deeply moving. Hartsfield, he said, was "direct, forthright, with great foresight into the basic needs of man . . . he was a man ahead of his time."

In the memorial booklet printed for the funeral was Stephen Spender's poem, in tribute to "those who were truly great, . . . who, from the womb remembered the soul's history . . . who in their lives fought for life . . . born of the sun they traveled a short while toward the sun, and left the vivid air signed with

their honor." Graham Jackson, who had played his accordion
with tears in his eyes as President Roosevelt's coffin passed by,
played with equal emotion for his old friend Hartsfield. The se-
lections were those Hartsfield himself had said he wanted, fine
old Baptist hymns—"In the Garden," "When the Roll is Called
up Yonder," "I Know That My Redeemer Liveth," "Hills of
Home," "The Holy City."

Men who had given Hartsfield strong support, personal, financial, and political, over the years—and some few who had
fought him bitterly—all were crowded in the pews of the little
chapel, before massed floral tributes that filled the sanctuary.
Burial was in West View, and the pallbearers read like a who's
who of Atlanta's leaders in all fields. Among them were Robert
Woodruff, J. Paul Austin, William Bowdoin, Jesse Draper, L. W.
Robert, John Sibley, Jack Delius, Ray Nixon, Herbert Jenkins,
George Blount, and Professor Thomas Harrold, in whose home
at Winterville, Georgia, Hartsfield and Tollie had been married. Others were Abe Goldstein; C. O. Moon, associated with
Hartsfield in business enterprises; and his friend and neighbor,
banker Freeman Strickland. Charlie Brown, perennial political
opponent, was there. Everett Millican, lifelong friend; John
Portman, the rising young architect who had brought into being much of what Hartsfield had dreamed of, the skyline of a
great modern city; Republican Rodney Cook, whom Hartsfield
admired; State Representative Kil Townsend; realtor T. M.
Alexander; and Muggsy Smith, who had hoped that Hartsfield's
mantle as mayor would fall on him—all were there, each with
his own memories.

There were no blacks among the pallbearers, but the black
community was well represented by Vice-Mayor Maynard Jackson, Jesse Hill, the insurance man, and the Reverend Martin
Luther King, Sr. Hartsfield had locked horns with the Fulton
County Commission in many battles in the past, but former
commissioners James Aldredge and Walter Mitchell were there

to pay him tribute. Mayor Sam Massell and former mayor Ivan Allen were honorary pallbearers, and the directors of the Southeastern Fair Association, of which Hartsfield was president, made up the honorary escort at the burial service in West View.

Present at the graveside with Tollie and Hartsfield's adopted son, Carl, were his son, William Hartsfield, Jr., and his daughter, Mildred Hartsfield Cheshire. One not present, but whose heart was there, was Pearl Williams Hartsfield. Feeble now, and nearly blind, she had attended the funeral in the chapel, sitting unrecognized in the crowd. Not feeling strong enough to make the long ride to the cemetery, she was taken home to Pelham Road. Soon thereafter she moved into a nursing home, where in 1972 she died, still wearing the gold wedding band Hartsfield had given her, still remembering the few happy years they had known together before he had given his life over completely to a city and its people.

EPILOGUE

EVER A MAN to preen and bask when the spotlight was upon him, Hartsfield would have richly savored the praises heaped upon him by press and public at his passing. *Time* magazine said of him that he had "influenced the city's development more than any person in modern times,"[1] which would have pleased him, for it is what he had set out to do, and he once had said so but in other words. The *Constitution* editorial on the day after he died pointed out that a reporter once had asked him to write his own obituary. Without blinking, Hartsfield replied, "You can start off by saying 'He pulled Atlanta kicking and screaming into the mid-20th century.'"[2]

That was true, the editorial continued, listing all that he had done—the fiscal reform, the development of Atlanta as a great aviation center, the construction of Buford Dam to assure Atlanta a steady water supply, the Plan of Improvement that tripled the size of the city and amounted to a reorganization of Atlanta and Fulton County government, and finally his masterful handling of the racial situation through a coalition of black and white voters. And in accomplishing all these, he was never dull and sombre, but full of life and fun.

The editorial concluded: "Hartsfield was a colorful con man in his way, a great promoter, a man who could breathe life into any cause he believed in . . . He brought strength and vitality and intelligence to everything that interested him. He loved politics and people and his city. We liked him, and we admired him and we will miss him."

To Jack Spalding, editor of the *Atlanta Journal:* "Bill Hartsfield was a fighter, he fought all his life. He came up the hard way and his nature was contentious. He didn't always fight because he had to, he fought because he liked it. He would win his fights not by force of logic but by sheer force. He would move up on his opponent, leaning over him if the opponent was short. His big blue eyes would bulge and shine. His index finger would advance. The words were torrential." Hartsfield, Spalding pointed out, was not only a fighter, he was an actor and promoter, and he combined these talents to make a great politician, able to "overpower and overwhelm." One of his greatest assets, too, was his common sense. "This resulted in the airport being ready when the jets were ready, in expressways commenced before the days of federal largesse and in the end of black political slavery here." "These three things," Spalding said, "have done more for the good of Atlanta than 100 Forward Atlanta Campaigns."

Bill Hartsfield's burden was that of all Southern politicians. He would have made a magnificent governor or senator or congressman. But what was right for Atlanta wasn't right for the rest of the state and the state lost great leadership because of that. His understanding of the future and his failure to reverence the past was the great good luck of Atlanta. Certainly he would have been willing to share his extraordinary political acumen and gifts with a state which needed them the worst way. But he was never asked and he was too smart to offer.

In being faithful to his constituency, to the needs of Atlanta, Bill Hartsfield lost the chance for higher office just as Richard Russell lost the presidency by remaining faithful to the Georgia of his youth.

With luck we're seeing the end of those days. Bill Hartsfield was a tremendous force in breaking these shackles. He was ahead of his time most of his life.[3]

The *Atlanta Journal* titled its eulogy "The Old Master," and

Hartsfield would have found no fault in this appellation. Nor with the *Journal's* conclusion: "It is impossible to separate Atlanta and Bill Hartsfield. Both are intertwined. Each contributed to the other success and without him there is going to be a vacancy difficult, if not impossible, to fill."

The spoken word was equally eloquent. On WAGA television Ray Moore said: "Mr. Hartsfield was no phony. He had a hot temper and let it explode. He had a great sense of humor, a great zest for life. He could and did get depressed and to those close to him he didn't try to hide that, either, but he always bounced back with optimism and hope, and renewed energy. For much of his life he poured all of that into a devotion to Atlanta. And the quality and energy of his life are embedded forever in this city."

Groups honored his memory. In Los Angeles, city council stood a moment in silent tribute to the man who had been the mayors' mayor. In Atlanta the Georgia House of Representatives, whose motives regarding Atlanta Hartsfield had always questioned, officially expressed its grief. Governor Jimmy Carter said that "his death brought sorrow not only to Atlanta but to all Georgia, . . . even those whom he engaged in bitter controversy respected him for his sincere concern for the people of his city." Mayor Sam Massell said that "Atlanta will miss Hartsfield forever. He is irreplaceable." Later, on June 8, this same thought was expressed by John Mayson, of the Atlanta Gas Light Company, as in front of City Hall a shining light began to glow in Hartsfield's memory.

Time magazine in its obituary noted that for all his services to the city only two things up to that time had been named for Hartsfield—a baby ape and a garbage incinerator. Mayor Sam Massell soon remedied this oversight. On the day Hartsfield would have been eighty-one, March 1, 1971, city council passed an ordinance saying that the Atlanta airport was the product of William B. Hartsfield's energy, enthusiasm, and talent, and that henceforth it be known as the William Berry Hartsfield Airport. Six months later Massell went on step further. He unveiled at the airport a bas-relief in honor of Hartsfield and proclaimed that henceforth the name should be the William Berry Hartsfield International Airport.

In a graceful speech Tollie Hartsfield accepted the plaque and the new name, which she said "made immortal the Hartsfield years." She expressed her love and gratitude to all who had made it possible, and the phrase she used—that the act of dedication made Hartsfield's deeds "immortal"—was not overdrawn.[5] For it meant that so long as airplanes flew, and Atlanta welcomed the traveler from around the world, the name of Hartsfield would be read in the papers and heard on the air every day—a reminder of what the great city towering on the horizon owed to him, and he to it.

NOTES

INTRODUCTION

1. Stephen Vincent Benét, "Notes to Be Left in a Cornerstone."
2. W.B.H. to Kathryn Johnson, AP reporter, in *Athens Banner-Herald*, August 14, 1960.

CHAPTER 1

1. H. W. Grady to Boston Merchants' Association, December 1889; quoted in J. C. Harris's *Life of H. W. Grady* (New York: Cassell Publishing Co., 1890).

CHAPTER 2

1. Jean Martin, *Mule to Marta* (Atlanta Historical Society, 1976).
2. From a 1934 political brochure sponsored by McDuffie supporters.
3. *Atlanta Constitution*, August 8, 1936.
4. Ibid.
5. *Atlanta Constitution*, September 24, 1936; quoted by Franklin M. Garrett in *Atlanta and Environs* (1954; rpt., Athens: University of Georgia Press, 1969) 2:945.
6. Ibid., p. 958.
7. W.B.H. to Woman of the Year Dinner, January 21, 1944.
8. Richard B. Harwell, ed., *Margaret Mitchell's "Gone with the Wind" Letters, 1936–1949* (New York: MacMillan, 1976), p. 284.

9. W.B.H. to David O. Selznick, 1939.

10. W.B.H. on wsb radio, 10:30 P.M., November 8, 1939.

11. Harold Martin, *Atlanta Georgian*, December 16, 1939.

12. Willard Cope, *Atlanta Constitution*, December 16, 1939.

13. Selznick's telegram and letter and the note from the Gables are among a number of letters and telegrams of appreciation that Hartsfield received from Hollywood personalities in December 1939. All are now in Special Collections at the Robert W. Woodruff Library, Emory University.

14. Report by officers Clous and Visscher dated July 27, 1940.

15. W.B.H. to G. C. O'Dell, Fifth Ward committeeman, November 8, 1940.

16. W.B.H. to Celestine Sibley, *Atlanta Journal-Constitution* magazine section, December 10, 1961.

CHAPTER 3

1. *Journal Magazine*, June 7, 1942.

2. Special message from W.B.H. to city council, June 1, 1942.

3. W.B.H. to city council, January 6, 1941.

4. H. H. Gibson to George B. Lyle, January 22, 1942.

5. W.B.H. to Major John T. Carlton, October 22, 1942.

6. W.B.H. to Mrs. Helen W. Cox, State Board of Pardon and Parole, June 29, 1945.

7. W.B.H. to Martin Dies, March 13, 1944.

8. W.B.H. quoted by Herbert Jenkins in 1976 interview with author.

CHAPTER 4

1. Bishop Gerald P. O'Hara to W.B.H., June 1946.

2. Speech by W.B.H. at Saint Joseph's Dinner, Ansley Hotel, April 24, 1946.

3. W.B.H. to Palestine Resistance Committee, March 14, 1947.

4. W.B.H. to John W. Hazard, staff editor, *Kiplinger Magazine*, July 12, 1947.

5. Author, in altercation with Hartsfield, 1940.

6. John T. Carlton, *Journal Magazine*, July 9, 1939.

7. W.B.H. to M. H. Ackerman, postal inspector, Atlanta, Ga.

8. W.B.H. to Ken Turner, October 30, 1945.

9. W.B.H. to Eugene Cox, January 6, 1945.

CHAPTER 5

1. W.B.H. to Druid Hills Baptist Church, February 1, 1948.

2. Undated [1948] city council resolution in tribute to Robert Woodruff.

3. Letter from J. H. Carmichael, Capitol Airlines, to W.B.H., May 10, 1948.

4. W.B.H. to city council, January 1946.

5. W.B.H. to city council, January 1947.

6. Ibid.

7. Mary E. Campbell, Saint Anthony's Catholic News, to W.B.H., September 1949.

8. Helen Bullard to W.B.H., September 1949.

9. John T. Carlton to W.B.H., June 20, 1949.

10. W.B.H. to Jimmy Dobbs, April 13, 1949.

11. *Atlanta Constitution*, August 13, 1949.

12. W.B.H. talk at Plaza Park, August 12, 1949.

CHAPTER 6

1. W.B.H. to city council, January 3, 1950.

2. Ibid.

3. W.B.H. to city council, January 3, 1951.

4. W.B.H. to NAACP convention, July 6, 1951.

5. Editorial, *Atlanta Constitution*, July 11, 1951.

6. Reprint of *Pittsburgh Courier National* edition of July 7, 1951.

7. Luther Spinks to W.B.H., September 10, 1951.

8. Aubrey Milam to W.B.H., January 1952.

9. W.B.H. to city council, January 3, 1952.

10. *Atlanta Constitution*, February 26, 1952.

11. *Atlanta Constitution*, December 3, 1952.

CHAPTER 7

1. Ralph McGill to Ben Hibbs, August 4, 1953.
2. *Atlanta Journal Magazine,* December 12, 1953.
3. W.B.H. to board of aldermen, January 4, 1954.
4. W.B.H. to L. F. Brown, Lewis Historical Publishing Co., January 29, 1954.
5. W.B.H. to board of aldermen, January 3, 1955.
6. Ibid.
7. John Pennington in *Atlanta Journal,* August 6, 1955.
8. W.B.H. to M. B. Burke, executive director of Barnum and Bailey and Ringling Brothers Circus, December 13, 1955.
9. W.B.H. to Kenneth Nix, July 13, 1956.
10. Dr. Mason T. Lowance to W.B.H., December 20, 1955.
11. Citation, Emory Special Collections.
12. Ed Hughes interview with W.B.H., *Atlanta Journal,* December 9, 1956.
13. C. B. Culpepper, speech at Hartsfield's birthday party, March 1, 1957.
14. Helen Bullard in interview with author, January 1977. Also Joe Cumming, *Atlanta* magazine, November 1961.
15. *Atlanta Constitution,* May 10, 1957.
16. Quoted by Ed Hughes, *Atlanta Journal,* September 13, 1957.
17. *Atlanta Journal,* December 3, 1957.
18. *Atlanta Constitution,* December 5, 1957.

CHAPTER 8

1. W.B.H. to board of aldermen, January 6, 1958.
2. *Atlanta Journal,* October 13, 1958.
3. Ibid.
4. Letter from Dwight D. Eisenhower to W.B.H., October 20, 1958.
5. Bob Greene, *Newsday* profile, October 1958.
6. *Atlanta Journal,* July 8, 1958.
7. *Atlanta Journal,* July 31, 1958.
8. W.B.H. to board of aldermen, January 5, 1959.
9. Quoted by Ed Hughes, *Atlanta Journal,* January 3, 1959.

10. Ed Hughes, *Atlanta Journal,* January 5, 1959.

11. Quoted by Marion Gaines, *Atlanta Constitution,* speech of W.B.H. to Fifth District Junior Chamber of Commerce at Atlanta Elks Club, January 3, 1959.

12. Curtiss Driskell, *Atlanta Journal,* February 13, 1959.

CHAPTER 9

1. Undated draft of William Emerson report to *Newsweek* magazine, published October 10, 1959; also quoted in *Atlanta Constitution,* October 13, 1959.

2. Ibid.

3. W.B.H. to board of aldermen, January 4, 1960.

4. Letter from George Goodwin to W.B.H., October 5, 1959.

5. Letter from W.B.H. to Pearl Williams, June 4, 1910.

6. Author's interview with Helen Bullard, April 1977.

7. Ivan Allen, Jr., with Paul Hemphill, *Mayor: Notes on the Sixties* (New York: Simon and Schuster, 1971).

8. Joseph Cumming, "Last Hurrah for Hartsfield," *Atlanta* magazine, November 1961.

9. *Atlanta Journal,* June 7, 1961.

10. Eugene Patterson, *Atlanta Constitution,* June 8, 1961.

11. Quoted by Pat Watters, *Atlanta Journal,* June 9, 1961.

12. Pat Watters, *Atlanta Journal,* January 3, 1962.

13. Letter from W.B.H. to Ivan Allen, December 21, 1961.

CHAPTER 10

1. Author interview with Tollie Hartsfield, April 1977.

2. Ibid.

3. *Atlanta Constitution,* March 30, 1962.

4. Quoted by Pat Potter, *Atlanta Constitution,* April 29, 1962.

5. Hartsfield's comments in the following paragraphs are taken from the minutes of the Ford Foundation Committee on Review and Evaluation of Urban Programs meeting, April 26, 1962 at the University of Illinois.

6. W.B.H. to Robert Woodruff, January 2, 1963.

7. Quoted by Walter Rugaber, *Atlanta Constitution,* April 7, 1963.

8. Eugene Patterson, *Atlanta Constitution*, May 13, 1963.

9. Quoted by Tollie Hartsfield in interview with author, August 1976.

10. Quoted by John Pennington, *Atlanta Journal*, August 14, 1964.

11. Quoted by Raleigh Bryans, *Atlanta Journal*, February 12, 1964.

12. Ibid., November 24, 1963.

13. *Atlanta Journal*, July 17, 1965.

14. Telegram from L.B.J. to W.B.H., July 2, 1964; letter from W.B.H. to L.B.J., July 2, 1964.

15. Caughey Culpepper to W.B.H., January 14, 1965.

16. W.B.H. to Caughey Culpepper, January 14, 1965.

17. W.B.H. to editor, *Saturday Review*, April 8, 1965.

18. W.B.H. to Paul Austin, April 23, 1965.

19. W.B.H. to Elmer George, Georgia Municipal Association, February 4, 1965.

20. W.B.H. to Pollard Turman, February 22, 1965.

21. Letter from Martin Luther King, Jr., to W.B.H., March 15, 1965.

22. *Atlanta Journal*, April 4, 1965.

23. M. M. Melson to W.B.H., October 15, 1958.

24. W.B.H. to Robert Woodruff, February 26, 1966.

25. Ann Carter, *Atlanta Journal-Constitution*, July 9, 1967.

26. Celestine Sibley, *Atlanta Constitution*, September 15, 1966.

27. Quoted by Joe Brown and Marion Gaines, *Atlanta Constitution*, October 4, 1966.

CHAPTER 11

1. Quoted by Wayne Kelley, *Journal-Constitution* Washington correspondent, April 5, 1967.

2. W.B.H. on WSB, January 24, 1967.

3. Quoted by Jesse Outlar, *Atlanta Constitution*, May 12, 1967.

4. Quoted by Jim Minter, *Atlanta Journal-Constitution*, June 11, 1967.

5. Robert Woodruff to W.B.H., May 23, 1968.

6. *Atlanta Constitution*, March 28, 1968.

7. W.B.H. to James S. Pope, February 9, 1968.

8. W.B.H. to Spiro Agnew, October 31, 1969.

9. *Atlanta Journal,* April 10, 1968.

10. Robert Rohrer, *Atlanta Constitution,* July 4, 1969.

11. W.B.H. to Charlie Leftwich, June 3, 1969.

12. Benjamin Mays to W.B.H., July 26, 1969.

13. Benjamin Mays, *Born to Rebel* (New York: Scribners, 1971).

14. Quoted by David Massey, *Atlanta Journal,* August 8, 1969.

15. Letter from W.B.H. to Dixie Dowis, January 30, 1970.

16. W.B.H. to Georgia senators and congressmen, May 13, 1970.

17. W.B.H. to Henry Bowden, June 18, 1970.

18. Author interview with Tollie Hartsfield, January 1977.

EPILOGUE

1. "Milestones," *Time,* March 8, 1971.

2. *Atlanta Constitution,* February 24, 1971.

3. Jack Spalding, *Atlanta Journal,* February 24, 1971.

4. *Atlanta Journal,* February 23, 1971.

5. Remarks by Tollie Hartsfield at airport ceremony, December 10, 1971.

INDEX